Pauline Amieurff

NAMING THE ROSE

NAMING THE ROSE

DISCOVERING WHO ROSES ARE NAMED FOR

ROGER MANN

PHOTOGRAPHY BY YVONNE ARNOLD AND PAUL BARDEN

EBURY
PRESS

CONTENTS

BEAUTIFUL ROSES FOR . . . *211*

HOW TO GROW ROSES *243*

to Yvonne,
for the music and the roses

'COMTESSE VANDAL'

Paul Barden

INTRODUCTION

Offer someone a rose, and almost always the first thing they'll do is smell it. It's such a common gesture that we are apt to forget how intimate it is, this raising the flower to the face and with eyes closed breathing in its sweetness. So perhaps it's not surprising that often as not the question will be asked, what is its name?

Not what sort of flower it is; there can be very few people who would not recognise a rose. It's a request for an introduction: of all the roses in the world, which one is this? Often its raiser will have named it to evoke its beauty and the joy that roses can bring to those who grow and admire them; and sometimes those names are touched with poetry – 'Crimson Glory', 'King's Ransom', 'First Love', 'Tendresse'.

Equally often it will bear a person's name, for the breeding of roses is an art and like all artists the raisers of roses enjoy dedicating their creations to people they love or admire. We might never have heard of these people otherwise, but every such rose – 'Lorraine Lee', 'Mme Hardy', 'Cécile Brunner' and all the rest – is a silent witness to a story of love and friendship. And what rose lover hasn't raised one of them to his or her face and wondered what its story might be?

That is what this book is about. Some of our stories are simple ones: of a parent's love for a child, of a man's for his wife or mother – private stories perhaps, but in whose joy the rose invites us to share. Others tell of men and women who have touched the pages of history, if only for a little while, and who have been deemed worthy of the honour of having their names immortalised by the beauty and fragrance of a rose.

Every European language calls the rose by some variation of the Latin name *rosa* – which in turn derives from the Greek *rhodon* – and Juliet would have had to travel far to find a different name for the flower. Perhaps to Persia, in whose language it is *gül*, a name that also stands for all flowers, as though the rose epitomised them all; to China, where the rose is known as *qiangwei*; or to Japan, where the name is *bara*.

The roses of China and Japan were to transform the roses of our gardens almost beyond recognition, but that was not till long after Shakespeare's day. The roses he knew all bloomed once a year, as spring turned to summer, and the different varieties didn't have names so much as descriptive titles – the Red Rose, the Great White Rose, the Maroon Velvet Rose or the Thornless Virgin Rose. Some, following a tradition that goes back to the ancient Romans, were designated by their place of origin, such as the Damask Rose, which was said to have come from Damascus, or the Great Holland Rose, which was a relative newcomer. It was also known unromantically as the Cabbage Rose or in Latin as *Rosa centifolia*, the rose with a hundred petals; but whatever you called it, it was the sweetest-scented of them all.

It is tempting to speculate that Shakespeare had it in mind when he wrote those words – but most flowers had different names in England and on the Continent or even according to a local nurseryman's fancy.

> What's in a name? That which we call a rose.
> By any other name would smell as sweet.
>
> *Shakespeare*

This didn't matter much when even the best-stocked nursery could offer fewer than twenty roses and new ones came on the market only very rarely. Roses are long-lived and easy to propagate from cuttings, and while new varieties can be grown from seed few people bothered. Like fruit trees, roses don't 'breed true' from seed and the seedlings are almost always inferior to their parents. Even today rose breeders estimate that, for every new rose they introduce (all its plants the progeny of a single seed), some five or even ten thousand seedlings have been grown, tried out for five years or so, and then rejected.

It's a costly exercise, and it wasn't until almost the end of the eighteenth century that the discovery of the sexuality of plants enabled plant breeders to make planned cross-pollinations and sow pedigreed seed, or that sufficient demand for new roses arose for rose breeders to make a living.

In the meantime, the great Swedish botanist Carl Linnaeus (1707–78) had reformed the scientific names of plants and animals, and it was he who determined that botany would call the rose by its accustomed Latin name *rosa*. He suggested that new species be named

'LA REINE VICTORIA', PARENT OF 'MME PIERRE OGER'

in honour of deserving scientists, but only a handful of the 150-odd known species of rose have been so named, and then not until quite late in the nineteenth century. Examples are *R. brunonii* and *R. moyesii*.

Then at the very end of the century the Empress Joséphine of France (1763–1814) brought roses into the height of fashion. She took her gardening seriously and her gardens at the Château de Malmaison near Paris were a major centre of botanical and horticultural research. It is said she introduced over 200 new plants to French gardens, among them the dahlia and the bougainvillea; but roses were her great love. She collected every variety then known, and to display them better she gave them a garden to themselves.

The Malmaison rose garden was the first devoted to a single flower since the Romans had planted terraces with violets, and its descendants still adorn parks and public gardens the world over. Its impact on the fashionable world of the day was immediate. Henceforth no self-respecting garden owner could be without a 'rosarium' of his or her own, however modest, in which to show off a selection of the very latest varieties.

These the French rose growers were more than willing to create, with such success that

'CATHERINE MCAULEY'

Yvonne Arnold

they dominated rose breeding up to the eve of the First World War; the great majority of what we now know as the Old Garden Roses are of French origin and bear French names.

And they created them in ever-increasing numbers. In 1791, M. Filassier, a leading Paris nurseryman of the day, could offer only 25 roses. Joséphine herself had about 250 in her collection; but in 1829 – only fifteen years after her death – the catalogue of M. Desportes listed 2,562. At the end of the nineteenth century one expert estimated that no less than 30,000 new roses had been raised and introduced, in literally dozens of new classes born of marriages between the newly introduced roses of the Orient and the established roses of Europe. Heaven knows how many have been added since!

Most of these roses have dropped out of the catalogues, victims of changing fashion or (whisper it) their own mediocrity; but even in these days, when few nurseries can afford to offer long lists of varieties, a diligent searcher of catalogues can choose from some 4,000 roses in Australia alone. World-wide the number is at least three times that, with over a hundred new ones being introduced every year.

With so many new roses jostling for attention, it must have quickly become obvious that the old descriptive titles would no longer suffice. Something more glamorous than 'Double Pink' was called for – and how many ways are there to say it anyway, even if you added your own name by way of trademark as some eighteenth-century nurserymen had done? (Though when Mr Shailer of Bath named his 'Shailer's White Moss' in 1790 he no doubt felt as entitled as any artist to sign his masterpiece.)

This is not to say the raisers didn't come up with names that suggested the excellent qualities of their roses. They did (and still do), and charming examples may be found in any catalogue. One mustn't overdo it, however. The now-forgotten raiser of 'Queen of Perpetuals' must have cringed when he read what the great English rosarian William Paul thought about it. His description consisted of the single word 'worthless'. As for the more recent 'Model of Perfection' – it isn't!

The Dutch tulip fanciers of the early seventeenth century had faced a similar problem, and they hit on the idea of naming their creations after local notables, perhaps in the hope that these gentlemen would be vain enough to pay the huge prices the latest striped tulips could command. Closer to home, French chefs had long been in the habit of dedicating their new creations to their patrons, and why should the creators of roses not do the same?

Why indeed, but not for them the serried ranks of admirals and consuls and Roman emperors of the tulip beds. The gallant French preferred to dedicate their roses to women; and while many men have been honoured with fine roses, the ladies outnumber them to this day. It is appropriate they should, for is not the rose the most feminine flower in the world?

They named their creations for their aristocratic patrons and for the celebrities of the day – writers, artists, generals and politicians (and their wives), even for the heroes or heroines of the latest plays or operas.

As rose growers still do; but we should beware of seeing such dedications as merely what modern marketing people would call 'celebrity endorsements'. Sure, a famous name can help create interest in a new rose; but in the end a rose wins its place in the catalogues and in our hearts on its own beauty and merit. And if it does, it gives its dedicatee a kind of immortality. It's hardly surprising that to have a rose bear your name is considered a great honour.

The celebrity whose secretary curtly informed the American raiser Ralph Moore that her boss 'was not endorsing any products at this time' missed out badly. Mr Moore named the rose 'Rise 'n' Shine' instead, and it has had a long career as the leading yellow miniature rose.

Then there is the often-told story of 'Mrs Lovell Swisher', a pink hybrid tea raised by Howard and Smith in 1926. Mr Swisher was a Californian businessman and he and his wife were leading members of the Garden Club of America – but before the ink was even dry on the catalogues she ran off with the chauffeur! Her furious husband demanded the name be withdrawn, but it had already been registered and could not be changed. So he spent $20,000 buying up every plant he could get his hands on. None of it is true, the Lovell family has testified. There was no adultery, no divorce, and no frantic buying up and burning of rosebushes. Lucy and Lovell Swisher remained happily married all their lives, and 'Mrs Lovell Swisher' is still available in America. It's an attractive rose, though we might wonder how many people have bought it for a giggle!

The roses in this book have been selected for their merit and fame as roses, and it is striking how often the famous (and not so famous) people whose names they bear have turned out to be rose lovers or at least keen garden lovers – and often friends or personal acquaintances of the raiser. They have earned the honour by their devotion to the Queen of Flowers, and naturally the raisers have always honoured those who have devoted their whole lives to her service, their own wives and families and those of their colleagues. Theirs are some of the most beautiful roses in the catalogues, for any man wishes to give those loves only the best – and a rose-grower's family can hardly help becoming good judges of roses anyway.

'DIANA, PRINCESS OF WALES'

Yvonne Arnold

Yet of all the people of the rose, these – Mme Pierre Oger, Maman Cochet, Mme Lauriol de Barny and the others – are the most tantalising. We may know who their husbands were, but it has often been difficult to find their own names, let alone a picture. (Don't forget that until the invention of cheap portable cameras made home-made photographs possible, having your portrait taken meant the expense of a trip to either a painter's or, later, a photographer's studio.)

From our standpoint in the early twenty-first century, we may feel that the dedication to Madame Jacques So-and-So is really a dedication to Jacques himself and that the gallantry doesn't ring quite true: but well into the twentieth century a respectable married woman was known to all but her most intimate friends by her husband's name. The rosarian's wife stood beside him, certainly, but her own life was private. Still, that doesn't stop us asking whether she was as beautiful as her rose – of course she was! – and imagining her quiet life among the roses, with the world's turbulent wars and politics only rumbles on the horizon. It must have been a satisfying life, too; many of the big names in rose breeding today are families who have been growing and breeding roses for generations.

There were times when the convention of naming the rose for the wife must have been convenient for the raiser. Patriotism might suggest a rose to honour the new president or prime minister but that might be too much of a political statement for some customers. His wife would be safer!

The turn of the twentieth century saw the arrival of raisers from other countries – Britain, Germany, the United States, Denmark, Australia – to challenge the dominance of the French. With the advent of 'plant patents', first in the USA in 1930 and then in most other countries – Australia took its time over this, 'plant variety rights' only becoming available in 1987 – raisers could now earn royalties on their roses wherever they were sold, not just on those sold through their own catalogues.

This made the market an international one, and it led to a new problem over the choice of names: a name that appealed in the home market might not be so well received in others. American gardeners in particular disliked foreign names, which they found difficult to pronounce; and as the American market is a huge one, much changing of names occurred, to the confusion of rose lovers everywhere.

It was the practical French, led by Alain Meilland, who proposed the solution now generally adopted. When a new rose is registered (the International Registrar for Roses is the American Rose Society) it is given an international codename or 'international variety name' whose first three letters are always those of the raiser – MAC for McGredy, KOR for Kordes and so on. This is constant, no matter what name a rose might be known by in different countries, and if you read about a must-have rose in a foreign magazine or on the internet it's worth checking its codename. You may have it already! In theory the codename should be quoted whenever a rose is described in a catalogue or in a book, but I have generally omitted it here. Only recent roses have codenames in any case.

Another recent development is the 'sponsorship' of new roses, the purchase of the naming rights to a new rose for a fee commensurate with the raiser's cost in raising it. This is often done by companies or charities for advertising purposes – the rose is endorsing them rather than the other way around! – and they often choose to name their rose after their founder or chief executive or his wife. But anyone can sponsor a rose, and if you'd like to have a rose named after someone you love, your first call should be your local rose society, who can put you in touch with a raiser or two.

What of the future? We may be sure that new roses will be raised, that they will be beautiful, and that the dedication of a rose will still be a high honour. It is an honour that cannot be compelled (to the credit of the German raisers, no rose was ever dedicated to

Hitler or his cohorts) and we may hope the raisers in whose gift it lies will continue to resist any political and commercial pressure to bestow it on the unworthy.

Reviewing the roses selected for this book, both those whose stories have been told at some length and the equally desirable ones that could only be given a short entry, it strikes me that there is nobody among their dedicatees whom I would not be delighted to meet. They have come from many countries and from all walks of life; but they live together in the rose garden in beauty and harmony. If only all the people and nations of the world could learn to do the same.

> I don't know whether nice people tend to grow roses
> or growing roses makes people nice.
>
> *Roland A. Beowne*

PEOPLE OF THE
ROSE

Abraham Darby

Modern shrub, David Austin (UK), 1985.
Large full-petalled flowers in blends of pink and apricot,
borne all season on an upright bush. Strong fragrance.

'Named on behalf of the Ironbridge Museum Trust after one of the founders of the Industrial Revolution', the raiser tells us. In fact there were three men who qualify for the honour: Abraham Darby (1678–1717), whose pioneering use of coke in his furnaces at Coalbrookdale in Shropshire first allowed the making of cheap cast iron; his son Abraham (1717–63), who made the cast-iron boilers for the first steam engines; and his son, also Abraham (1750–91). He was the brilliant engineer who in 1779 built the elegant cast-iron bridge (the first in the world) over the Severn near Coalbrookdale from which the trust, dedicated to the preservation of Britain's industrial heritage, takes its name.

So here we have a rose that honours not just one person but three. And as though aware of this rare distinction it varies both in colour – from pure apricot to warm rose-pink – and in form, from loose and cup-shaped to the full quartering shown in Paul Barden's photograph. The bush is compact, without the tendency to become a climber that affects some of Mr Austin's 'English roses' in warm climates. Growth is bushy and healthy.

Strict Quakers, the Darbys refused to have their portraits taken, though legend says the silhouette of a man's face the sharp-eyed see in the iron keystone of the Iron Bridge is that of Abraham III. That's it at the top of the page.

2

Paul Barden

3

Yvonne Arnold

Albertine

Climber, Barbier et Cie (France), 1929.
Soft warm-pink, medium-sized flowers borne in clusters in late spring
with a few later on a vigorous plant. Delicious fragrance.

Hampered by poor translations, English-speaking readers are apt to find Marcel Proust's vast and rambling novel *À la recherche du temps perdu* (*Remembrance of times past*) rather heavy going. The French, however, rightly consider it a masterpiece; and when M. Barbier brought out 'Albertine' they would have immediately recognised its name as that of Proust's beautiful heroine, Albertine Simonet.

Barbier was indeed a great admirer of Proust and it is said he originally wished to dedicate this rose to the memory of the author, who had died in 1922. But another raiser had already used the name (for a rose now forgotten), so he had to be content with Albertine – and as he had already called his own daughter Albertine, the rose honours both the fictional young lady and the real-life one named after her. Proust would have smiled; and he would have appreciated Barbier's choice of a rose so feminine in colour and romantic in scent.

'Albertine' remains a universal favourite, and recently Henri Delbard has honoured Proust's memory with the vigorous and very sweetly scented yellow 'Souvenir de Marcel Proust'.

5

Alister Stella Gray

Noisette, Alexander Hill Gray (UK), 1894.
Smallish buff-yellow to ivory flowers, borne in sprays all
season on a robust climbing plant. Very good fragrance.

Stella is a most unusual name for a boy, but Alexander Gray (1837–1929) had very good cause to bestow it on his son and to use the lad's full name when he dedicated this really excellent climbing rose to him. His adored young wife Stella had died in childbirth in 1877, and with her last breath she had asked him to name the baby after her.

> I went out into the garden in the morning dusk,
> When sorrow enveloped me like a cloud;
> And the breeze brought to my nostril the odour of roses,
> As balm of healing for a sick soul.
>
> *Moses Ibn Ezra (1060–1138)*

She is also remembered in 'Souvenir of Stella Gray', a 1909 Alex Dickson introduction in apricot and carmine; and two years later Dickson brought out 'Alexander Hill Gray', an exhibition rose in pale yellow that is still well worth growing. Both are teas, which must have delighted Mr Gray as he loved the tea roses above all others – so much so that in 1885 he sold up his ancestral estates in Scotland and moved south with his family to the kinder climate of Bath. He served for many years on the committees of the National Rose Society, whose members used to call him the King of the Teas. The French would have called him *un rosomane*, a man crazy for roses.

Yvonne Arnold

Anna Pavlova

Hybrid Tea, Peter Beales (UK), 1981.
Very large shapely flowers in delicate pink, borne all
season on a very tall bush. Intense fragrance.

The illegitimate daughter of a St Petersburg laundress, Anna Pavlova (1881–1931) was a sickly child; but she loved to dance and at ten entered the Imperial Ballet School, where her exceptional talent was quickly recognised. In 1899 she joined the Imperial Ballet, becoming prima ballerina in 1906; her most famous ballet, The Dying Swan, was created for her in 1907. After a spell with the Ballets Russes in Paris, she settled permanently in London in 1914 and formed her own company, which she took on several very successful tours around the world. She is the most celebrated ballerina of all time, but though the airy meringue-based dessert called pavlova was created in honour of her Australian tour of 1929 (or maybe in New Zealand), she never received the honour of a rose in her lifetime.

> If the rose puzzled its mind over the question of how it grew,
> it would not have been the miracle it is.
>
> *William Butler Yeats*

Mr Beales tells us that a friend writing Pavlova's biography fell in love with this superbly fragrant rose and asked him to dedicate it to her memory. He did; and though it has never received wide publicity, 'Anna Pavlova' is a first-rate rose, its only fault being its sky-scraping bush. Yvonne Arnold had to climb a stepladder to take the photograph.

Yvonne Arnold

Archiduc Joseph

Tea, Gilbert Nabonnand (France), 1892.
Large, informal flowers in coral rose shaded crimson,
borne almost all year on a tall bush. Very good tea-rose scent.

Joseph was a favourite name in the Habsburg royal family, and there have been several Archdukes Joseph. The best known nowadays is Joseph August (1872–1962), a prominent figure in Austro-Hungarian politics during and after World War I; but our rose honours his father, Joseph Karl (1833–1905), known as Joseph of Austria. The son of another Archduke Joseph, Joseph Anton, he was the brother of Maria-Henrietta, dedicatee of 'Duchesse de Brabant'.

> How fair is a garden amid the toils and passions of existence.
>
> *Benjamin Disraeli*

As Palatine of Hungary and Supreme Commander of the Hungarian army, he was a very important man, but following a quarrel with his cousin the Emperor Franz Joseph he decided in 1890 to quit politics and retire to his estate in Fiume (now called Rijeka) on the Adriatic coast and indulge his passion for music and gardening. His forte was palms, on which he was an acknowledged authority, but we may imagine him giving this splendidly masculine rose a place of honour in his garden, which is still maintained as a botanic garden by the Croatian government.

Don't confuse it (as is often done) with Pierre Bernaix's red-and-purple tea of 1891, 'Monsieur Tillier', named for the then director of the French National School of Horticulture.

Yvonne Arnold

André Marie Edouard

Louis Gaspard Aimédée

Baron Girod de l'Ain

Hybrid perpetual, Reverchon (France), 1897.
Cupped crimson blooms edged in white, borne in spring and
autumn on a tall bush. Strong damask fragrance.

The proliferation of barons and baronesses in France can be confusing for someone used to the British system in which there can only be one Baron So-and-So at a time. But when Napoleon recreated the French aristocracy he decreed that if a man ranked as a baron (it is not a particularly lofty rank) all the men in his family did too.

> Oh what a red mouth has the rose,
> The woman of the flowers
>
> *Leigh Hunt*

The Girod de l'Ain are one such aristocratic family and, as the raiser apparently didn't specify which Baron Girod de l'Ain he had in mind, you can choose your favourite: Baron Louis Gaspard Aimédée (1781–1847), whom Napoleon appointed to his Council of State at the age of twenty-nine and who enjoyed a distinguished career in politics for the rest of his life? Baron Félix Jean (1789–1874), one of Napoleon's generals and a raiser of merino sheep? The military historian Baron Maurice, born in 1854? Or, the most likely candidate, the garden-loving Baron André Marie Edouard Girod de l'Ain (1819–1906), the head of the family at the time? But the rose is unique, its only rival being the hard-to-grow 'Roger Lambelin' (Schwartz, 1890), named for a royalist politician.

Yvonne Arnold

Baroness Rothschild

('Baronne Adolphe de Rothschild') Hybrid perpetual, Jean Pernet (France), 1868.
Large soft pink flowers borne freely in spring and autumn
on a compact bush. Little fragrance.

Grandson of Meyer Rothschild, the founder of the Rothschild banking dynasty, Adolphe de Rothschild (1823–1900) originally ran the Rothschild bank in Naples. In 1850 he married his cousin Julie von Rothschild (1830–1907) and in 1855 they acquired and rebuilt the Château de Prégny in Geneva to house his celebrated collection of works of art. In 1860 he moved his bank to Geneva, and in Prégny's gilded salons and among the trees and flowers of its vast gardens overlooking the lake, Baroness Julie played hostess to half the crowned heads of Europe. No doubt they also partied aboard her steam yacht *Gitana*, which captured the world water speed record (21.5 knots!) in 1876.

> ... and she was the loveliest little thing one could imagine,
> as tender and fair as the most beautiful rose-leaf
>
> *Hans Christian Andersen*

Life wasn't all parties. Returning by train to Geneva one day, Baron Adolphe got a cinder from the engine smokestack in his eye, and in gratitude to the young surgeon who saved his sight he founded Switzerland's first eye hospital in 1874, ordering that all patients be treated free of charge for a century. After his death, Baroness Julie endowed the Adolphe Rothschild Foundation in Paris, which remains in the forefront of ocular research. Her rose remains one of the great Victorian roses.

Yvonne Arnold

Baronne Edmond de Rothschild

Hybrid tea, Marie-Louisette Meilland (France), 1967.
Cyclamen pink and white bi-coloured flowers borne
all season on a tall bush. Strong fragrance.

Popular with exhibitors for its perfect form and with the rest of us for its distinctive colour and fine scent, this rose was named during the festivities celebrating the twentieth anniversary of the Geneva International Rose Trials to mark the long-standing support given to the trials by Baron Edmond de Rothschild (1926–97) and his wife Nadine (1932–).

Nadine de Rothschild (née Lhopitalier; she married the baron in 1962) is a woman of many talents: sometime actress (she made twenty-eight films under the pseudonym Nadine Tallier), successful novelist, and widely read writer on matters of taste and etiquette, what the French call *savoire-vivre*. And she's a garden lover. The gardens at her Château de Prégny have long been famous, and recently she and her son Maurice bequeathed the whole property to the city of Geneva.

Also a keen gardener, Baron Edmond was a financier, a major underwriter of the state of Israel, a property developer, and one of the founders (and a major shareholder) of the resort chain Club Méditerranée; but he was also a notable philanthropist, endowing hospitals, museums and cultural events – and of course the Rose Trials.

Yvonne Arnold

Yvonne Arnold

Baronne Prévost

Hybrid perpetual, Jean Desprez (France), 1842.
Large lilac-pink flowers borne in spring and autumn on
a sprawling, thorny bush. Rich damask fragrance.

One of the oldest hybrid perpetuals in the catalogue but still a splendid rose – and a fine example of how a rose can keep alive the memory of someone otherwise forgotten.

Who was she, this baroness? All we know is that she was the sister of a friend of the raiser, one Eugène Guenoux, who bred dahlias in a pretty village called Voisenon, about 40 kilometres up the Seine from Paris; and that she married the Baron Prévost, scion of an ancient family that had provided France with a *Maréchal* or two and a governor-general of French Canada.

May we imagine M. le Baron visiting the local nursery to buy plants for the garden of his country estate, falling in love with the beautiful Mlle Guenoux, and making her his baroness? Did his family approve of the match? The baron's distant cousin, the novelist the Abbé Prévost, might have told us in a tale of true love blossoming among the flowers, but he had died in 1763.

Basye's Purple

Rugosa hybrid, Robert E. Basye (USA), 1968.
Medium-sized single purple flowers borne all season
on a tall, spreading shrub. Sweet fragrance.

It is an unwritten rule, very rarely broken, that a raiser never dedicates a rose to himself. That would be like a general awarding himself a medal. But it is an artist's privilege to sign his work with pride! He can hardly inscribe his name on the leaves, but he can give his rose a name like 'McGredy's Yellow' or 'Rouge Meilland', following a tradition going back to the eighteenth century. And though little-known, 'Basye's Purple' is a rose any raiser would be proud of – healthy and handsome in growth, free in bloom and unique in colour, which varies from the crimson-purple of a young burgundy to startlingly pure violet.

Dr Robert Basye (1908–2000) would argue that breeding roses is both an art and a science. He was a professor of mathematics who for fifty years raised roses as a hobby, his dream being roses immune to black spot. To this end he made a particular study of rose genetics and brought hitherto unused species such as 'Basye's Purple's' parent *R. foliolosa* into his breeding lines. His work continues: in his will he endowed a Chair in Rose Genetics at his old institution, Texas A&M University.

Beauty is an ecstasy; it is as simple as hunger.
There is really nothing to be said about it.
It is like the perfume of a rose: you can smell it and that is all.

W. Somerset Maugham

Paul Barden

21

Yvonne Arnold

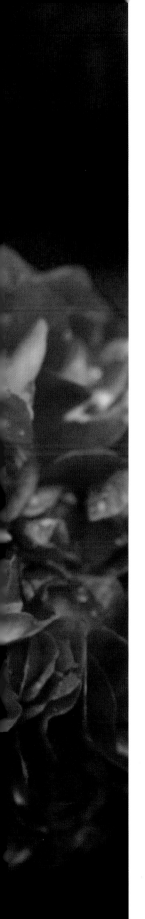

Belle de Crécy

Gallica, Roesser (France), 1828.
Shapely, old-fashioned flowers blending pink, violet and mauve
borne freely on a twiggy bush in spring. Superb scent.

The legend has grown up that the name of this rose, one of the most admired of the purple gallicas, honours Jeanne-Antoinette Poisson, Marquise de Pompadour (1721–64), mistress of Louis XV, whose country house was the Château de Crécy-Couvé near Dreux. Some have gone so far as to declare that it was raised there by her gardeners.

Alas, sober history holds that 'Belle de Crécy' was raised in 1828 by one M. Roesser, a nurseryman of Crécy-en-Brie, and suggests that he meant the name (Beauty of Crécy) simply as a compliment to his home town, then a country village but now engulfed by the eastern suburbs of Paris. But 'belle' is ambiguous – even in English we may call a beautiful woman 'the belle of the ball' or 'the belle of the village' – so who can say for certain that M. Roesser did not have the beautiful chatelaine of Crécy in mind? Mme de Pompadour is known to have loved roses, and her exquisite taste was responsible more than anyone's for the flowering of artistic talent that has made *Louis Quinze* a byword for elegance. She is certainly worthy of being remembered by a rose as fine as this.

Bettina

Hybrid tea, Francis Meilland (France), 1953.
Shapely orange flowers borne all season on
an average-height bush. Light fragrance.

Top fashion models are international celebrities today, but it was not always so. Until the 1950s, they were just anonymous clotheshorses.

The girl who changed all that, the first star model, was the petite redhead Bettina Graziani (1925–) known professionally simply as Bettina. The daughter of a Normandy schoolteacher, she moved to Paris at the age of eighteen, hoping to become a fashion designer; but her beauty and unstudied poise soon attracted the eye of Jacques Fath, whose favourite model she became. 'Dior may have his New Look, but Fath has Bettina,' quipped the fashion pundits, and indeed her picture was in every magazine.

When Hubert de Givenchy, another Fath protégé, set up his own salon in 1952 Bettina joined him as his chief model and director of publicity. For her he created the iconic white cotton 'Bettina blouse' – and for her Francis Meilland named this stylish rose, one of the first roses of its colour.

In 1955, at the height of her fame, she met Prince Ali Khan and gave up her career for love; but when he was killed in a car crash in 1960 she returned to fashion, now as a manager, a writer and, yes, as a designer. She still looks terrific in her eighties.

Fashion may change, but beauty never!

Thomas Rivers

Yvonne Arnold

Bishop Darlington

Hybrid musk, George C. Thomas (USA), 1926.
Apricot to cream flowers borne all season in sprays on a tall
spreading shrub or short climber. Sweet scent.

The hybrid musks are chiefly associated with the English raiser the Reverend Joseph
Pemberton (1852–1926), who pioneered the class and coined its name. He named many
after heroines of Greek and Roman legend – 'Penelope', 'Cornelia', 'Thisbe' – but Captain
Thomas preferred to honour an old family friend, James Henry Darlington (1856–1930),
the Episcopal bishop of Harrisburg, Pennsylvania.

> The wilderness and the solitary place shall be glad;
> and the desert shall rejoice and blossom as the rose
>
> *Isaiah 35: 1*

Consecrated in 1905, Bishop Darlington is remembered as 'a man of high culture,
deeply religious and deeply humane'. Loved as a spiritual leader and philanthropist, he
was a tireless worker in the cause of Christian unity, a poet whose verses are still in print,
a lover of music – at a time when many saw jazz as the work of the Devil, he invited jazz
musicians to play in his cathedral – and a pioneer conservationist. His role in the creation
of Pennsylvania's first wilderness parks is remembered by the section of the Appalachian
Trail that bears his name.

His rose is a double tribute, first to the good bishop himself and second to the American
Rose Society, whose headquarters were then in Harrisburg. Not one of those roses that
screams out loud for attention, it is worthy of the honour.

Yvonne Arnold

Blush Noisette

Noisette, Phillippe Noisette (USA), 1815.
Smallish palest-pink flowers, borne freely all season on a
bushy climber or large shrub. Sweet musk-rose scent.

The life of Philippe Stanislaus Noisette would make a great movie. He was the son of Louis XVI's head gardener, and when the Revolution broke out in 1789 he emigrated to Haiti. Then Haiti also suffered a revolution and in 1794 he took his wife Célestine and their six children to Charleston, South Carolina. There he established the first specialist rose nursery in America; but Célestine was an African-American and South Carolina law did not recognise inter-racial marriage. This Noisette refused to accept, and after years of litigation he succeeded in having his marriage and children legitimised.

His business flourished, for thanks to his stay-at-home brother Louis, now one of France's leading rose growers, he had the most up-to-date catalogue in America. He returned the favour: first with a pink climber named 'Champneys' Pink Cluster' after a customer called John Champneys who had raised it from a cross of the musk and China roses, and then in 1814 with a rose he had raised from its seed and which he called simply 'Blush'. Louis added the family name, and 'Blush Noisette' created a sensation. The first repeat-blooming climber ever, it gave birth to a new class of roses, the noisette roses – the only class to originate in America.

Yvonne Arnold

Rosa brunonii

Rambler, introduced from Nepal in 1822.
Big sprays of smallish white flowers borne in spring on a very
vigorous climbing plant. Strong sweet fragrance.

Brunonius is Latin for brown – the Scottish army surgeon turned botanist Robert Brown (1773–1858), a protégé of Sir Joseph Banks. Australians remember him as Matthew Flinders' naturalist on his epic 1801–05 circumnavigation of Australia, during which Brown made the greatest contribution to our knowledge of the flora of the island continent of any single botanist. Back in Britain, he served as Banks' librarian and assistant, and on Banks' death in 1820 became first Keeper of Botany at the British Museum. In the quiet of his laboratory, he developed new and improved methods of classifying plants; in 1827 he discovered the important phenomenon of physics known as Brownian motion; and about five years later he discovered that each living cell contains a nucleus.

The Jupiter of Botany, his colleagues called him; and it is fitting that his rose with its greyish-green leaves should be one of the mightiest of climbing roses, quite capable of mounting the top of a forest tree to wreathe it in spring with a cloud of scented flowers and in autumn with cascades of small glittering hips.

> I saw the sweetest flower wild nature yields,
> A fresh-blown musk rose ...
> ... and as I feasted on its fragrancy
> I thought the garden rose it much excelled.
>
> *John Keats*

Yvonne Arnold

Cara Bella

Floribunda, Frank Riethmuller (Australia), 1960.
Small apple-blossom pink flowers in large sprays all season on
a spreading, almost thornless shrub. Fruity fragrance.

The name is officially spelt as one word, 'Carabella', and when the rose was still quite new I asked the raiser what it signified, as I couldn't find that word in the dictionary.

'Can you keep a secret?' the old man said. 'It's named after a dear friend and neighbour of mine who is too modest to allow me to give her name to a rose. Her family has always called her Bella, Italian for 'the beautiful one'; and so I dedicated the rose in Italian to dear Bella, 'Cara Bella'. You know her: she's one of our Rose Society's show judges, Mrs Marsden. But don't tell her I told you.'

That was over forty years ago, and now that 'Cara Bella' is enjoying renewed popularity for its simple wild-rose charm and its ease of culture, perhaps the secret of its name may be revealed. (And yes, even in middle age she was a beautiful woman.) Prune lightly and allow the autumn flowers to ripen their round orange hips.

If love were what the rose is
And I were like the leaf,
Our lives would grow together,
In sad or singing weather,
Blown fields or flowerful closes,
Green pleasure or grey grief.

Algernon Charles Swinburne

Yvonne Arnold

Cardinal de Richelieu

Gallica, Jean Laffay (France), c.1845.
Medium-sized rich purple flowers borne in late spring on a
tall bush with smooth mid-green leaves. Sweet scent.

Pedants may object that the cardinal's hat bestowed in 1622 upon Armand Jean du Plessis, Duc de Richelieu (1585–1642) was not purple but scarlet; but M. Laffay must have felt – and rosarians have agreed ever since – that his rose's rich and glorious colour was ecclesiastical enough to commemorate the great statesman who was the real ruler of France during the reign of Louis XIII and whose consolidation of the power of the monarchy paved the way for the glories of the reign of Louis XIV. His methods might not be thought politically correct today, but he was a deeply cultured man, the founder of the Académie Française and a patron of science.

> They are not long, the days of wine and roses:
> Out of a misty dream
> Our path emerges for a while, then closes
> Within a dream.
>
> *Ernest Dowson*

He was a notable gardener too, not that Edward Bulwer-Lytton depicts him gardening in his play *Richelieu*, written in 1838 and all the rage in Paris in the early 1840s. It is remembered today for the single line 'the pen is mightier than the sword', but its title role attracted many of the great actors of the nineteenth century, notably the American Edwin Booth (1833–93), older brother of the ne'er-do-well John Wilkes Booth who assassinated President Lincoln.

Paul Barden

Catherine McAuley

Floribunda, Jack Christensen for Jackson & Perkins (USA), 1993.
Large golden yellow flowers in small clusters all
season on an average-height bush. Mild scent.

A rose which though bred in the US is currently only available in Australia. Perhaps because it dislikes very cold winters, Jackson & Perkins decided not to market it at home; but their Australian agent Valerie Swane liked its shapely flowers, clear unfading colour and prolific plant. It was 'sponsored' by the Sisters of Mercy and named for their founder, the Venerable Catherine McAuley (1778–1841).

> Every rose is an autograph from the
> hand of God on his world about us.
>
> *Theodore Parker*

Her father, a Dublin builder, inspired Catherine to dedicate her life to helping the poor; but she was orphaned at an early age and it wasn't until she was forty that an inheritance from her foster-parents enabled her to found the first House of Mercy dedicated to social work among poor and disadvantaged women. Encouraged by the Archbishop of Dublin, she founded the Sisters of Mercy in 1831. Within ten years there were twelve Mercy convents in the UK; the first in Australia was established in Perth in 1846. Today the Sisters run schools, hospitals and orphanages all over the world. As Catherine intended, each establishment is entirely self-governing and it was not until 1994 that the umbrella organisation Mercy International was formed. Our rose celebrates that event.

Yvonne Arnold

Cécile Brunner

Polyantha or hybrid china, Joseph Pernet-Ducher (France), 1881.
Small pale-pink flowers borne in sprays all season
on a shortish bush. Light fragrance.

'Cécile Brunner' is one of the best-loved of all roses, and it is pedantic to insist on the original name 'Mlle Cécile Brunner'. Still, that might stop people calling it Cecil Brunner, thereby subjecting 'the charming daughter of M. Ulrich Brunner, rose-grower of Lausanne' to the indignity of a sex-change – at the age of two! – and spoiling the young M. Pernet-Ducher's graceful tribute to a senior colleague and rival.

The exquisite perfection of its little flowers has always made this a favourite rose for bridal bouquets and corsages – hence its American nickname the Sweetheart Rose – and we may feel sure that Cécile herself carried it on the day she married Paul Willmann of Geneva, where her father had moved his nursery in 1892. They had a son, Jean.

Pernet-Ducher's original is a compact bush, but there is also a very much bigger-growing version (a sport) which bears its blooms in great airy sprays of as many as a hundred. Almost identical in leaf and flower (though it usually extends one sepal into a small leaf), it goes by the name 'Bloomfield Abundance', though some nurseries carelessly sell it as 'Cécile Brunner'. Check those sepals when you buy!

The delicate curve of petals standing out
in relief, like the eyelids of a child.

Auguste Rodin

Yvonne Arnold

Yvonne Arnold

40

Chapeau de Napoléon

Centifolia, Jean-Pierre Vibert (France), 1827.
Medium to large rose-pink flowers borne in late spring
on a tallish bush. Heavenly fragrance.

In view of the impetus that Napoléon (or rather his wife Joséphine) gave to rose growing in France, it is surprising that this is the only rose bearing his name that has come down to us – and it is named not so much for the emperor himself as for the way its unique pine-scented, crested sepals suggest the outline of his famous tricorne hat.

At least they do to French rose lovers. The American rosarian Robert Buist (writing in 1844) makes the apt comparison with the luxuriant moustaches favoured in his day; and the English have always preferred to call it the 'Crested Moss' or *R. centifolia cristata*. Nor does it date from Napoléon's time; Vibert is said to have found it in a convent garden in Switzerland in 1825. No matter: by whatever name you call it, this is a very beautiful rose, and its scent is unsurpassed. It does best in cool climates and may need a discreet stake or two to correct its rather floppy habit.

Charles de Gaulle

('Katherine Mansfield') Hybrid tea, Marie-Louise Meilland (France), 1974.
Large shapely lilac flowers borne all season on
a tallish bush. Excellent fragrance.

Soldier, leader of the Free French resistance to the Nazis during World War II, leader of the government after Libération (1944–46) and President of France from 1958 to 1969, Charles de Gaulle (1890–1970) is one of the leading figures in twentieth-century French, indeed European, history. So it was hardly exaggerated patriotism on Meilland's part to dedicate a rose to his memory in the year Paris's Charles de Gaulle Airport opened.

President de Gaulle's chauvinism didn't always endear him to foreigners, especially in the South Pacific where he insisted on testing France's nuclear weapons. So it's perhaps not astonishing that New Zealand rosarians prefer to call his rose by the name of one of their own heroes, the writer Katherine Mansfield (1888–1923), one of the great masters of the short story. The daughter of a Wellington businessman, she spent most of her life in Britain; but many of her finest stories draw on her memories of her childhood in New Zealand. Some may feel that this softly coloured and sweetly scented rose – one of the best mauve HTs – is more appropriate for her than for a gruff old soldier.

An idealist is one who, on noticing that a rose smells better than a cabbage,
concludes that it will also make better soup.

H.L. Mencken

Yvonne Arnold

Charles de Mills

Gallica, date and raiser unknown.
Medium-sized flowers in crimson and purple, borne in late
spring on a medium-height bush. Sweet scent.

'Charles de Mills' is deservedly one of the most admired of all the old garden roses, but all we know of its provenance is that it was re-introduced under this name from the collection of antique roses at the Roseraie de l'Hay near Paris in the early twentieth century. Who raised it and when we do not know.

And who was M. de Mills? A rose-loving Englishman called Charles Mills, a director of the British East India Company no less, who lived in Italy in the 1740s? Another Charles Mills who was born in 1873 and enjoyed a career as a concert pianist in America? A nineteenth-century German rose lover, one Charles Wills? Or did the battered old label at the Roseraie actually read 'Charles Le Moyne', as has been suggested recently? Nineteenth-century rose books do speak of a purple rose of that name, and we know who he was – a member of a prominent family of French nurserymen, the Lemoines of Nancy, who are famous for their lilacs and peonies. But contemporary descriptions of that rose don't quite fit. Does it really matter, as long as we have his rose?

Mystery glows hidden in the rose bed,
Secrets lie hidden in the rose.

Farid un-din Attar

Paul Barden

Charles Mallerin

Hybrid tea, Francis Meilland (France), 1947.
Very large shapely flowers in deepest velvet red, borne all
season on a very tall bush. Wonderful fragrance.

The most beautiful red rose ever raised, and a worthy tribute from the great Francis Meilland to the man who had taught him the art of breeding roses. But it is a temperamental performer, apt to be lanky in growth, stingy with its wonderful flowers and resentful of any but the lightest pruning.

In this, it is almost a portrait of its dedicatee. Charles Mallerin (c.1890–1960) was a Swiss central-heating engineer who retired early so he could devote himself full-time to his hobby of breeding new roses. Some of the most beautiful roses of the 1920s, '30s, '40s and '50s are his, and he ranks as the greatest amateur raiser ever. The rose world recognised his genius, but they also told tales of his prickliness. Like the time he won both the gold and silver medals at the Concours de Bagatelle. Any other raiser would have expressed his humble thanks, but not M. Mallerin. From his home in Grenoble he wrote to the Bagatelle chairman informing him that he must rescind the awards and give the silver medal winner the gold and vice versa. 'Your judges are completely ignorant! They know nothing of roses!'

Oh lost green Paradise,
Were the roses redder there,
Than they blossom other where?

Christina Rossetti

46

Yvonne Arnold

Mrs H.Evans

Commandant Beaurepaire

Bourbon, Moreau-Robert (France), 1874.
Large flowers striped in red, violet and white, borne freely in spring
and sparingly later on a tall, arching bush. Rich fragrance.

Had Nicolas-Joseph Beaurepaire (1740–92) lived in normal times, history would have forgotten him. He entered the French army in 1757, advanced to the rank of colonel, and retired with a chestful of medals in 1791.

But his were not normal times. Following the French Revolution, Prussia and Austria declared war on the new republic and Colonel Beaurepaire was called from retirement to defend – with only a few hundred ill-trained conscripts – the strategically important town of Verdun in Lorraine. In September 1792 a Prussian army of 60,000 under the Duke of Brunswick laid siege to the town. The mayor and council, even Commandant Beaurepaire's own officers, urged surrender; but rather than sign the papers he shot himself, crying 'I prefer death to life under despots!' Verdun surrendered (the French retook it two months later) but Beaurepaire was hailed as a hero and given a state funeral and a tomb in the Panthéon.

After France's inglorious defeat by Prussia in the Franco-Prussian War of 1870–71, she sorely needed heroes, and Beaurepaire was freshly honoured with the dedication of statues, streets and city squares all over France – and with this most gorgeous of all the old striped roses.

Comte de Chambord

Portland, Moreau & Robert (France), 1860.
Medium-sized, full-petalled rose-pink flowers borne all
season on a compact bushy plant. Rich fragrance.

Henri, Comte de Chambord (1830–83), is one of the tragic figures of French history. He was the grandson of Charles X, the last Bourbon king of France; and when in 1871 Napoleon III's Empire collapsed following the French defeat in the Franco–Prussian War, the National Assembly offered him the crown. But he insisted that the red-white-and-blue *tricolour* be replaced as the national flag by the old white flag of the Bourbon kings, and to this the Assembly and the people would not consent. The Assembly thereupon proclaimed the Third Republic, and Chambord returned to the exile in which he had lived almost all his life.

When Moreau and Robert dedicated 'Comte de Chambord' to him in 1860, these events still lay in the future and many people then must have looked forward to his coronation as King Henri V. Its compact growth, fine scent and abundant repeat bloom make it one of the best antique roses for the small garden. However, some pundits insist that the rose we have is actually one raised in 1859 by Joseph Boyau of Angers and named 'Mme Boll' after the wife of a Swiss colleague, Daniel Boll, who had moved to New York where he specialised in roses and camellias.

Flowers leave their fragrance in the hand that bestows them.

Chinese proverb

Mrs H.Evans

Comtesse Vandal

Hybrid tea, M.P.H. Leenders (Netherlands), 1931.
Large, warm pink flowers borne all season on an
average-height bush. Tea-rose fragrance.

The story goes that sometime in the late 1920s Leenders had won first prize for a display of his new roses in Paris. His trophy was a silk cushion exquisitely painted with a design of roses; and at the celebration dinner that evening the Comtesse Vandal remarked that here the artist had surely surpassed nature.

> It is at the edge of a petal that love waits.
>
> *William Carlos Williams*

Comte Albert Vandal (1853–1910) had been a historian, member of the Académie Française and a Chevalier of the Legion of Honour. In the 1920s, his widow would have been in her mid-sixties and a *grande dame* of Parisian society. Was she a member of the exhibition committee, maybe even the one who selected the painted cushion? Was she serious, or was she just indulging in a little banter over the champagne with a man young enough to be her son?

History does not say, but Leenders rose to the occasion magnificently.

'Madame, I accept your challenge. I shall create a rose to surpass these painted flowers – and it shall bear your name!'

And so he did: when 'Comtesse Vandal' made its debut it was hailed as 'the most artistic bloom in Rosedom'. It might claim that title still. Many rosarians think it is best grown today in its excellent climbing version.

Paul Barden

Constance Spry

Modern shrub, David Austin (UK), 1961.
Large old-fashioned rose-pink flowers borne in late spring
on a tall shrub or moderate climber. Strong, spicy scent.

The daughter of a railway clerk, Constance Spry (1886–1960) spent her early years in Ireland, where she studied nursing. After an unhappy first marriage she moved to London to become a teacher of home economics. She married Henry Spry in 1921, and in 1929 left teaching to open an up-market flower shop in Pimlico. Not that she called herself a florist: she was a 'floral decorator', an apt title as her ideas on flower arrangement were fresh and original.

She taught her wealthy customers (and, through her many books, the world) to discard stiff bunches for graceful arrangements designed for the rooms they were to adorn, and incorporating such unorthodox materials as autumn grasses, sprays of woodland berries, decorative vegetables and the old garden roses – the gallicas, damasks, moss roses, bourbons – that she adored but which, at the time, were in almost complete eclipse.

Her example did much to restore them to favour, and when David Austin created this, the first of his new old-style roses (and still one of the most beautiful despite its lack of repeat bloom), it was a happy thought to dedicate it to her memory. It bears fine hips in autumn.

A flowerless room is a soulless room, to my way of thinking;
but even one solitary little vase of a living flower may redeem it.

Vita Sackville-West

Paul Barden

Crown Princess Margareta

Modern shrub, David Austin (UK), 2000.
Large flowers in apricot and peach, borne all season on a
tall shrub or short climber. Strong tea-rose scent.

This is one of the most admired of David Austin's recent roses, a fitting tribute to the lady they called the Flower Princess.

She was Queen Victoria's granddaughter Princess Margaret of Connaught (1882–1920), known to her family and friends as Daisy. When she met Prince Gustav Adolph of Sweden in 1905 it was love at first sight, and the prince's grandfather, King Oscar II, gave them Sofiero Castle near Helsingborg as a wedding present. There they created one of the most beautiful gardens in Scandinavia, and it is said that even royal visitors would find themselves invited to help with the weeding! Prince Gustav's passion was rhododendrons – for which Sofiero is still famous – but Kronprinsessan Margareta loved all flowers and the overall design of the garden is hers. During World War I she worked tirelessly for the Red Cross and the people of Sweden mourned deeply when their beloved Crown Princess died prematurely in 1920. She had borne her prince five children, and the present sovereigns of Sweden and Denmark are her grandchildren. Gustav became King Gustav VI Adolph in 1940 and on his death in 1973 bequeathed his beloved Sofiero to the citizens of Helsingborg.

She sped as Petals of a Rose
Offended by the Wind–
A frail Aristocrat of Time.

Emily Dickinson

Paul Barden

Crown Princess Mary

Hybrid tea, George Thomson (Australia), 2006.
Large pink and ivory flowers borne all season on
an average-sized bush. Light fragrance.

Royal weddings have often been celebrated with the dedication of a new rose to the bride, and that of Australia's Mary Donaldson and Crown Prince Frederick of Denmark in 2004 has proved no exception. Indeed the new Crown Princess has been honoured with two new roses, one raised in Denmark, the other in Australia.

> Just living is not enough ...
> One must have sunshine, freedom and a little flower.
>
> *Hans Christian Andersen*

The Danish one, 'Kronprinsesse Mary' (codename POULcas018) is a ground cover rose with full-petalled old-style flowers in soft yellow raised by the old and respected Danish firm of Poulsen Roser. The Australian one, 'Crown Princess Mary' (codename TOMroy) is the rose in the picture, a hybrid tea in a feminine blend of ivory and soft pink with a touch of apricot. Both are too new for a definite judgement on their merits, but they look very promising.

A few years ago it would have been unacceptable to give two different roses virtually identical names like this; but the adoption of the international codename system has meant that if any confusion arises you have only to check the codename to be sure which rose you have.

Yvonne Arnold

Dainty Bess

Hybrid tea, William Archer (UK), 1925.
Soft-pink flowers freely borne singly or in small sprays
all season on a tallish bush. Moderate fragrance.

'Dainty Bess' has always been the best-loved of the small tribe of single hybrid teas, and it is indeed a lovely thing, its only fault being a tendency for the bush to grow leggy. This is easily dealt with by planting it at the back of the bed; or you might prefer to grow the climbing sport, whose flowers are often larger and even finer.

Its raiser, William Archer, was a quietly unconventional man. At a time when most rosarians were besotted by big, many-petalled hybrid teas he appreciated the beauty of those with only five; at a time when most people pooh-poohed the old garden roses of the previous century his nursery offered a selection of the best; at a time when seemingly every other business was called So-and-So and Sons, he took his daughter Muriel into partnership and proudly headed his advertisements 'W.E.B. Archer and Daughter'. And when he came to dedicate the most beautiful of his roses to his wife, Elizabeth, he rejected the formal and socially correct 'Mrs W.E.B. Archer' or 'Mrs Archer' in favour of an open declaration of his love for his 'Dainty Bess'.

The roses under my window
make no reference to former roses or to better ones;
. . . There is simply the rose; it is perfect in every moment of its existence.

Ralph Waldo Emerson

Paul Barden

61

Dame Elisabeth Murdoch

('Speelwark') Hybrid tea, Reimer Kordes (Germany), 1999.
Large shapely flowers in yellow and pink, borne all
season on a tallish bush. Good scent.

Here we have a rose with a double dedication. English-speaking gardeners know it as 'Dame Elisabeth Murdoch' and in Germany where it was bred it is called 'Speelwark'.

Mother of the Australian–American media magnate Rupert Murdoch, Dame Elisabeth (1907–) is one of Australia's most notable philanthropists and patrons of the arts – and one of its leading gardeners too. Her Edna Walling-designed garden at Cruden Farm in central Victoria is widely regarded as one of Australia's finest, and she endowed the Chair of Landscape Architecture at Melbourne University.

> And I will make thee beds of roses
> And a thousand fragrant posies
>
> *Christopher Marlowe*

She is certainly worthy of her rose; but who, or what, is Speelwark? They are a folk-singing group from Reimer Kordes' hometown of Elmshorn in Holstein, little known to English-speaking audiences but very popular in Germany. They often perform medieval and renaissance folksongs, and when the music-loving raiser named the rose for them to celebrate their fifteenth anniversary, they were so delighted they wrote a song in High German about it (*Mein Roos*) and put its portrait on the CD cover!

Under either name this is a fine rose, one of the best and most distinctive yellow HTs of recent years. The amount of pink on its petals varies with the weather and the season.

Yvonne Arnold

Dr Van Fleet

Climber, Walter Van Fleet (USA), 1910.
Medium-sized pale-pink flowers borne in late spring on
a very strong climbing plant. Excellent fragrance.

When he was 18, Walter Van Fleet (1857–1922), the son of a country schoolmaster, ran away from home to work for a railway company in Brazil in the hope of studying the flowers of the Amazon. He was given little chance to do that and yellow fever nearly deprived America of its first internationally famous rose breeder.

On his return home he married his childhood sweetheart, Sarah Heilman, and became a doctor. But he had always wanted to breed plants, so in 1891 he forsook medicine and joined the US Department of Agriculture. For them he bred gladioli, strawberries, raspberries and blight-resistant chestnuts; but roses were his great love. He sought 'dooryard roses' which would flourish with little care anywhere; and of the many he raised, 'Dr Van Fleet' is his masterpiece. (He wanted to call it 'Daybreak' but was overruled.)

Then in 1930 a nurseryman in Connecticut noticed one of his plants of 'Dr Van Fleet' was flowering all season. It was propagated and introduced as 'New Dawn'. Less vigorous than its parent, 'New Dawn' is one of the world's favourite roses; but don't forget 'Dr Van Fleet'. If you want to slipcover the garage with roses, it would be a perfect choice.

Won't you come into the garden? I'd like my roses to see you.

Richard Brinsley Sheridan

Yvonne Arnold

Dorothy Perkins

Rambler, Jackson & Perkins (USA), 1901.
Sprays of small candy-pink flowers borne late in the spring
on a vigorous climbing plant. Little scent.

When Charles E. Perkins and his father-in-law, A.E. Jackson, founded the Jackson & Perkins firm in 1872, their plan was to grow grapes, and so they did for nearly thirty years. But then in 1900 one of their staff, Alvin Miller, raised a pretty candy-pink rambling rose and suggested that they market it: roses might be a profitable sideline. Of course it needed a name; and as Perkins' son George had just had a baby daughter it was decided to name it 'Dorothy Perkins' after her. (It seems she was named for her great-grandma Dorothy Jackson, so the rose is doubly honoured.)

The rest, as they say, is history. 'Dorothy Perkins' was an immediate hit – and Jackson & Perkins decided that henceforth they would specialise in roses. Before long they became the biggest firm of rose growers not just in America but in the world, a title they still claim. And despite its notorious addiction to mildew, 'Dorothy Perkins' is still a favourite, the archetypical rambler, one of those roses whose name every gardener knows. In 1986 the German raiser Karl Helzel announced a repeat-blooming version (a seedling, not a sport) with the faintly comical name 'Super Dorothy'.

> From fairest creatures we desire increase,
> That thereby beauty's rose might never die
>
> *Shakespeare*

Paul Barden

Duchess of Portland

('Portlandica') Portland, origin uncertain, c. 1780.
Medium-sized rose-red flowers borne in spring and
autumn on a compact bush. Moderate scent.

One of the first offspring of the marriage between European roses and the China rose, this attractive rose is also one of the oldest to bear a person's name – that of the beautiful Margaret Cavendish Bentinck (1715–85), one of the great eighteenth-century patrons of botany. The daughter of the wealthy and learned Duke of Oxford, she married the second Duke of Portland at the age of nineteen. It was a love match and she bore him five children, one of whom twice became prime minister. Their home, Bulstrode Hall in Buckinghamshire, was a showplace, the house filled with works of art (including the celebrated Portland Vase) and the garden with rare plants from all over the world, including roses. Every botanist of note was a regular visitor, and she is said to have preferred to talk plants with them at dinner than politics with her son's colleagues in the government. Alas, after her death her gardens fell into decay, her great collection of botanical books was dispersed, and the vase went to the British Museum. But her rose, the prototype of the portland roses, remains to delight us. Its origin is obscure, but some garden historians think it may have been raised in the rose garden at Bulstrode.

> If seeds in the black earth can turn into such beautiful
> roses, what might not the heart of man become in its
> long journey toward the stars?
>
> *G.K. Chesterton*

Yvonne Arnold

Duchesse de Brabant

Tea, H.B. Bernède (France), 1857.
Medium-sized flowers in clear soft pink, borne almost
all year on a tallish bush. Very good tea scent.

In the Middle Ages, the Dukes of Brabant were important figures among the rulers of northern Europe, but since the early nineteenth century their title has been borne by the Crown Prince of Belgium. The duchess of our rose is Marie-Henriette (1836–1902), born Archduchess of Austria and sister of the Archduke Joseph whom we have already met. She married Crown Prince Leopold (1835–1909) in 1853 and her beauty, charm and kindness immediately won her the love of her new people, who called her 'the Rose of Brabant'.

> You love the roses – so do I. I wish
> The sky would rain down roses, as they rain
> From off the shaken bush. Why will it not?
>
> *George Eliot*

But it was not a happy marriage. Leopold was not only physically unattractive but introverted and morose, and he was openly unfaithful to her. In 1865 he became King Leopold II; and while historians credit him with transforming Belgium into a modern industrial nation, he financed it by ruthlessly exploiting his personal fief of the Congo and treating its native people with such brutality that he was widely called the most evil man in Europe. Let us hope Marie-Henriette found some solace in the two roses named after her: the cherry-red climbing HT 'Reine Marie-Henriette' (Levet, 1878) and 'Duchesse de Brabant', one of the prettiest pink roses ever raised.

Yvonne Arnold

Edna Walling

Rambler, origin uncertain.
Semi-double pale-pink and white flowers borne in spring and
followed by red hips in autumn. Moderate fruity scent.

Writer, photographer, conservationist and landscape architect, Edna Walling (1895 –1973) is one of the most revered figures in Australian gardening. In a career spanning over forty years – from 1920 till the early 1960s – she created more than 300 gardens, many of which survive intact to enrich the nation's heritage. She always sought to adapt European traditions to the Australian climate and landscape and was one of the first designers to make use of native trees and flowers.

> The red rose whispers of passion,
> And the white rose breathes of love;
> O, the red rose is a falcon,
> And the white rose is a dove.
>
> *John Boyle O'Reilly*

Of course she planted roses also, and there are two bearing her name. The one you're more likely to come across in rose books is a sprawling shrub rose introduced in 1991 with sprays of rather ordinary small pink flowers, but this pretty rambler is much easier to find in the nurseries. It is believed to have been passed around by the owners of a couple of gardens in which she planted it in the 1940s, but where she got it from nobody knows. She would have loved its subtle shades of apple-blossom pink passing to pearly white and palest green – but plant it facing east or the hot afternoon sun will bleach them into dullness.

Yvonne Arnold

Elizabeth of Glamis

('Irish Beauty') Floribunda, Sam McGredy (UK), 1964.
Soft coral-pink flowers borne in clusters all season
on an upright bush. Very good fruity fragrance.

The dedicatee is of course Queen Elizabeth the Queen Mother (1900–2002), who was the daughter of the Earl of Glamis and spent her childhood at Glamis Castle in Scotland. (pronounced *glarms*) In 1923 she married Prince Albert, Duke of York, and the fragrant pink HT 'Elizabeth of York' (Dobbie, 1927) was a favourite in Britain for many years. With the abdication of Edward VIII in 1937, the Duke of York became King George VI and Elizabeth of York his Queen. During the war, her refusal to leave London even during the worst of the Blitz so boosted the morale of the British people that Hitler called this smiling lady in her fluffy hats and pastel dresses 'the most dangerous woman in Europe'.

> Observe this dew-drenched rose of Tyrian gardens.
> A rose today. But you will ask in vain.
> Tomorrow what it is; and yesterday
> It was the dust, the sunshine, and the rains.
>
> *Christina Rosetti*

A keen gardener since childhood and an avid rosarian, the Queen Mother (as she had become after her husband's death in 1952) became patron of the Royal National Rose Society in 1965. 'Elizabeth of Glamis' is said to have delighted her, and while not outstandingly disease-resistant it remains a very fine rose. In 1991 Reimer Kordes introduced the excellent cool pink floribunda 'Queen Mother' to mark Her Majesty's 90th birthday.

Yvonne Arnold

75

Ellen Tofflemire

Gallica hybrid, Paul Barden (USA), 2002.
Large, quartered flowers blending purple, mauve and violet,
borne in spring on a tall bush. Sweet fragrance.

Both in the kinds of roses he raises and in the names he gives them, a professional hybridist needs to keep his eye on the mass market. An amateur, on the other hand, needn't worry so much about profit and can afford to pursue out-of-the-mainstream breeding lines. Often this has spectacular results, such as this magnificent new gallica raised by Paul Barden, whose photographs adorn this book.

He has dedicated it to the memory of a close friend, the beautiful woman with whom he shared his photographic studio and who died tragically young in a car crash. It was she who first awakened his love of the old garden roses. Her rose may never sell in the millions – the market for new once-blooming roses is a niche one – but it is a worthy companion to the gallicas that have come down to us from the nineteenth century. In its combination of large size, perfect quartered form and astonishing range of colours, and in its unusually long period of bloom, it has few peers.

> The fairest things have fleetest end,
> Their scent survives their close:
> But the rose's scent is bitterness
> To him that loved the rose.
>
> *Francis Thompson*

Paul Barden

Empress Joséphine

Gallica hybrid, origin unknown.
Large rose-pink flowers washed with mauve borne
lavishly in spring on a tallish, almost thornless bush. Light fragrance.

They were a strangely matched pair, Napoléon Bonaparte and Joséphine Rose de Beauharnais – she the fascinating Creole from Martinique, thirty-three years old and a widow when they married in 1796; he the gruff young military genius from Corsica who rose to become Emperor of France and almost succeeded in becoming the master of Europe. She had known poverty, and when her husband's power brought her wealth she spent it lavishly – on clothes, on jewels and on the décor of her houses, but above all on indulging her life-long passion for flowers.

> The world is a rose; smell it and pass it to your friends.
>
> *Persian Proverb*

Her vast gardens and greenhouses at the Château de Malmaison blossomed with the rare plants of an empire, and the foremost botanists and artists were in attendance to study and record them; but her great love was the rose, the flower whose name she bore and which she brought into the very forefront of fashion. Her collection of some 250 varieties included every rose then known, including this one which she knew as *R. francofurtana*, the Rose of Frankfurt. It wasn't given her name until many years after her death in 1814, but we may be sure she would have approved. It is a very beautiful rose.

Paul Barden

Fantin-Latour

Centifolia, raiser and date unknown.
Large clear-pink flowers, shapely in the old style and
borne in late spring on a tallish bush. Superb fragrance.

Back in the 1920s and '30s when enthusiasts began collecting and distributing the old roses that had survived generations of public indifference, this rose turned up in several old gardens in Britain and America, always cherished for its tender colour and sweet fragrance but never with a name attached. It could hardly be reintroduced without one, and Graham Thomas proposed dedicating it to the great flower painter Henri Fantin-Latour (1836–1904).

His idea was eagerly taken up, though Fantin-Latour himself may have smiled. He is said to have regarded the shimmering flower pictures on which his reputation rests as mere bagatelles beside his many portraits, lithographs and salon pictures on operatic subjects.

> There is nothing more difficult for a truly creative painter
> than to paint a rose.
>
> *Henri Matisse*

There was, however, a dissenting voice from America, where the writer Ethelyn Emery Keays held that 'Fantin-Latour' is actually 'Céline', a 'hybrid bourbon' raised in 1835 by Jean Laffay and named, I believe, for his niece. She points out that in the 1870s it had been much used as an understock, which would account for its frequent but anonymous survival where it had suckered and smothered the rose budded on it. Maybe so, but rosarians are unlikely ever to divorce the great artist from his wonderful rose.

Yvonne Arnold

Yvonne Arnold

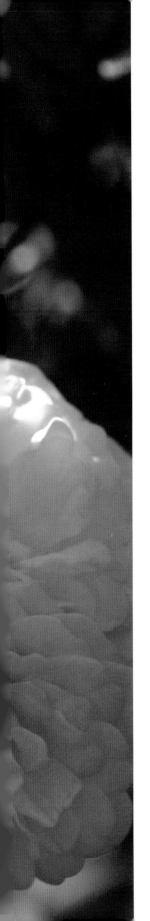

Félicité et Perpètue

Rambler, Antoine Jacques (France), 1827.
Sprays of small milk-white flowers in late spring,
on an almost evergreen climber. Delicate fragrance.

Don't let the name mislead you into thinking that this delightful rose
is perpetual-flowering. It isn't, though its display is both generous and
prolonged. It needs little pruning.

Its raiser was head gardener to the Duke of Orléans (later King Louis
Philippe of France), to whose daughter he had dedicated the blush-pink
'Adelaïde d'Orléans' in 1826. The story goes that he planned to name
his next rose to celebrate the birth of his own son – but Mme Jacques
presented him with twin daughters! As was the custom the girls were
duly given the names of saints: Perpetua and Felicitas, who suffered
martyrdom together at Carthage in 203 AD and who were invoked
together in the canon of the Latin mass. But the Church always gave
the noblewoman Perpetua precedence over Felicitas, a mere slave girl,
and it has been suggested that 'Félicité et Perpètue' may actually be
a misprint for 'Félicité Perpetuelle' (perpetual happiness). But might
not M. Jacques have deliberately given the names in reverse order to
emphasise that his rose honours not the martyrs but his two daughters?

A sport, 'Little White Pet' (Henderson, 1879) bears the same
flowers all season but on a dwarf bush.

Frau Dagmar Hastrup

Rugosa, Hastrup and Poulsen (Denmark), c.1914.
Clear pink single flowers borne all season and followed by red hips,
on a compact, very prickly shrub. Sweet scent of cloves.

This rose, whose compact habit makes it the best variety of *R. rugosa* for the small garden, poses a most unusual problem. We know who the lady was, but we aren't quite sure what her name was! She was the mother of the man who discovered the rose growing in a paddock in Denmark – but did she use the Danish form of her surname (Hartopp) or the German one, Hastrup? And was she Fru or Frau, the respective equivalents of Mrs? (Either way, the g in Dagmar is silent; pronounce the name *dah'mar*.)

Behind that question lies a thousand years of often bitter conflict between Denmark and Germany over the sovereignty of the border lands of the old Duchy of Schleswig-Holstein. The dispute was finally settled by a plebiscite a century ago, but there is still a German-speaking minority in southern Denmark, to which it appears she belonged. The great Danish rosarian Svend Poulsen (1884 –1974), whose father introduced the rose and who knew the lady, always calls her rose 'Frau Dagmar Hastrup' in his books. It has all the *rugosa* virtues of sweet scent, bushy growth and disease-proof foliage which colours up prettily in autumn. For a waist- to chest-high hedge it has no peer.

Yvonne Arnold

Yvonne Arnold

Frau Karl Druschki

Hybrid perpetual, Peter Lambert (Germany), 1900.
Very large, stark white flowers, borne in spring and
autumn on a tall bush. Almost no fragrance.

'Send this stiff, military-looking rose with no scent back to Germany or put her on the scrapheap!' thundered a writer in the 1916 *Rose Annual*. But British rose lovers weren't prepared to give up their favourite white rose merely for the Great War. They just changed its name to 'Snow Queen', which they argued was the original name anyway.

Which was true: Lambert had originally announced his wonderful white rose as 'Schneekönigin' after the Snow Queen of Hans Christian Andersen's fairytale. But tempted by the prize money, he entered it in a competition to select a rose to be named in memory of the German statesman Otto von Bismarck (1815–98).

It lost to a now-forgotten pink HT but won another contest held by the German Rose Society for a rose to honour the wife of their president, one Karl Druschki (1844–1902), a wealthy businessman with interests in the nursery trade. We may regret that Lambert didn't stick with the euphonious 'Schneekönigin'; but Frau Druschki was a leading rosarian herself and surely a more worthy dedicatee than the Iron Chancellor, who wasn't particularly interested in flowers. The rose itself remains unsurpassed.

Général Galliéni

Tea, Gilbert Nabonnand (France), 1899.
Informally styled flowers blending cream, pink and red,
borne almost all year on a tall bush. Mild fragrance.

One of the hardiest of the teas and though not very fragrant, a superb, free-blooming garden rose for mild climates, where it often blooms through the winter. In warm weather the open flowers are often entirely currant-red.

A veteran of the Franco–Prussian War, Joseph-Simon Galliéni (1849–1916) served with distinction in France's colonial wars in Vietnam and Africa. The rose was named to celebrate his appointment as Governor-General of Madagascar, in which role he gained a fine reputation for fairness and justice, but his greatest hour was to come in September 1914. He had been recalled from retirement to be military governor of Paris; and with the German army threatening the city and the regular French forces outnumbered, he organised a force of reservists and volunteers and sent them to the front in a fleet of commandeered taxis, the first use of the motor-car in warfare. The 'taxicab army', they called it – but it turned the tide of battle and Paris was saved.

It is said that on his deathbed he refused the honour of a tomb in the church of the Invalides, saying he preferred to lie beside his wife among the roses of a country churchyard.

There is material enough in a single flower
for the ornament of a score of cathedrals.

John Ruskin

Jocelen Janon

Général Jacqueminot

Hybrid perpetual, Roussel (France), 1853.
Large velvet crimson flowers borne in spring and autumn on
a tall bush; watch for mildew. Superlative fragrance.

Rose historians have been known to quip that Jean-François Jacqueminot, Vicomte de Ham (1787–1865) has won more fame in the rose garden than he ever did on the battlefield. There is truth in this, for 'General Jack', as it is affectionately known, is one of the all-time great roses. Practically every red rose in our gardens today descends from it, and it is still well worth growing if only for its legendary perfume.

> Great, glowing blossoms, holding in their hearts
> The garnered sweetness of unnumbered Junes …

> *Ednah Proctor Clarke*

But M. Jacqueminot's career was distinguished enough. At the age of eighteen he was commended for bravery at the Battle of Austerlitz, fought valiantly at Wagram, Essling and La Bérézina, and commanded a cavalry division at Waterloo. At the surrender he ordered his men to break their swords rather than hand them over, a gallant gesture that won the admiration of the victorious Duke of Wellington. Retiring from the army, he founded a silk factory in Bar-le-Duc that employed many of his old soldiers and, it is said, a brewery in Paris. He entered Parliament in 1827, becoming Vice-President of the Chambre des Députés ten years later and being put in charge of the National Guard in 1838. Ennobled in 1846, he retired from public life after the revolution of 1848.

Paul Barden

Georg Arends

Hybrid perpetual, Wilhelm Hinner (Germany), 1910.
Very large high-centred flowers in cool pink, borne
all season on a tall bush. Superb fragrance.

Astilbe × arendsii, Phlox × arendsii, Aconitum × arendsii . . . if you grow herbaceous perennials you can hardly escape the name of Georg Adalbert Arends (1863–1952) of Ronsdorf in Germany, one of the legendary plant breeders. His astilbes are perhaps the best known of the many fine plants that issued from his nursery – founded in 1888 and still run by his great-granddaughter Anja Maubach – but he also did notable work with kniphofias, hostas, sempervivums and sedums – the famous *Sedum* 'Herbstfreude' ('Autumn Joy') is one of his hybrids – and azaleas. He is remembered too by the Georg Arends Medal, the highest award in German horticulture.

Though not a rose breeder himself, he was a rose lover and in 1883 was one of the founders of the German Rose Society, the *Verein Deutscher Rosenfreunde*. And he was a pioneer of the modern style of growing roses with other flowers rather than always segregated in roses-only beds. So it is fitting that a rose should bear his name, and fitting that it should be one so glorious. 'Georg Arends' is rather more continuous in its flowering than most HPs, but like all its class it appreciates generous manuring and watering.

The fragrance always stays in the hand that gives the rose.

Hada Bejar

Yvonne Arnold

Ghislaine de Féligonde

Rambler, Eugène Turbat (France), 1916.
Soft yellow and pink flowers, fading to ivory. Abundant
late-spring bloom and scattered flowers later. Slight scent.

Often cited as an example of an ungainly name holding back a good rose – but pronounce it as the lady did (Helaine) and it's really quite melodious; and the rose, one of the few repeat-flowering ramblers, is a real charmer.

All flowers of all the tomorrows
are in the seeds of today.

Indian Proverb

It had not yet been named when it won the Certificate of Merit at the Bagatelle competition for new roses in 1915, and the award could not be finalised until it was. But at lunch that day the raiser heard the story then on all the lips of Paris, of how, some weeks before, the young Comte de Féligonde had been gravely wounded in battle and left lying in the no-man's-land between the armies where none of his comrades dared venture to save him; and how that evening his wife Ghislaine herself crossed the battlefield under fire, found him, dragged him to safety, and nursed him back to health.

The new rose, M. Turbat at once declared, had found its name: 'Ghislaine de Féligonde'. It is pleasing to record that Ghislaine and her husband lived to a happy old age – and that they were both rose lovers.

Paul Barden

Graham Thomas

Modern shyubrose, David Austin (UK), 1983.
Large deep yellow flowers borne all season on a tall,
sprawling bush. Very good spicy fragrance.

Nurseryman, writer, artist, musician and for twenty years garden adviser to the (British) National Trust, Graham Stuart Thomas (1909–2003) was one of the most influential rosarians of the twentieth century. Having decided at the age of eight to become a professional gardener, he trained at the Cambridge University Botanic Garden; and while his knowledge of plants of all kinds was immense, his great love was the old-world roses of the nineteenth century and earlier. Gathering them from gardens all over Britain and from France, he convinced the nurseries at which he worked to propagate and catalogue them. Their names had to be researched, their merits assessed, and their roles in modern gardens determined. All this he did; and his many books (some illustrated with his own delicate watercolours) established him as the world's leading authority on the subject.

When David Austin asked him to choose a rose to bear his name he chose this one, which he liked to describe as a nineteenth-century rose dressed in a twentieth-century colour. The first yellow Austin had raised, 'Graham Thomas' remains the most popular. In warm climates it grows very tall and may be treated as a short climber.

The rose looks fair, but fairer we it deem
For that sweet odour which doth in it live

Shakespeare

Yvonne Arnold

Handel

Modern climber, Sam McGredy (UK), 1965.
Medium-sized flowers in ivory and pink, borne in small clusters all
season on a moderately vigorous climber. Mild fragrance.

Everyone knows George Frideric Handel (1685–1759) as the composer of the 'Hallelujah Chorus'; but the master whom Beethoven called the greatest composer who ever lived has much more than that to his credit. The son of a Hamburg barber–surgeon who wanted him to become a lawyer, he lived for a while in Italy, managed an opera house in Germany, served as court composer to the Elector of Hanover, and finally settled in England. There he wrote Italian operas, oratorios in English, ceremonial music for the Court, and orchestral and chamber music as well as music for his own instrument, the harpsichord – music for every mood and feeling, all of it touched with that special beauty that musicians (for want of a better word) call Handelian.

And his connection with the rose? None, except that he is the music-loving Sam McGredy's favourite composer and this is one of his favourite roses. Though it often takes a couple of years to start climbing, 'Handel' is as fine an example as any of the modern style of climbing rose, restrained enough in vigour not to outgrow a small garden and flowering all season.

> Gather ye rosebuds while ye may:
> Old time is still a-flying;
> And this same flower that smiles today,
> Tomorrow will be dying.
>
> *Robert Herrick*

Yvonne Arnold

Harry Wheatcroft

('Caribia') Hybrid tea, Wheatcroft (UK), 1972.
Shapely flowers striped in red and yellow, borne all season
on average-height, upright bushes. Light scent.

The son of a Nottingham builder, Harry Wheatcroft (1898–1977) started his career as a motor mechanic. That didn't hold his interest, so he went to work for a firm which made lace, his home town's most famous product; but he got bored with that too so decided to join his brother David as a market gardener. That was more like it; but cabbages proved much less to his taste than roses. Before long the brothers had established themselves among Britain's leading rose growers, and Harry himself became one of Europe's best-known rose-men. He was famous not only for the parade of top-class roses the Wheatcroft firm introduced to the British public – including 'Peace' and 'Queen Elizabeth' – but for his socialist politics, his life-long pacifism (for which he had been jailed during World War I), his colourful clothes, and the magnificent mutton-chop whiskers which became his trademark.

> Full many a flower is born to blush unseen
> And waste its sweetness on the desert air ...
> ... but not if I can help it!
>
> *Harry Wheatcroft quoting Thomas Gray*

He could hardly escape being described as flamboyant, so it is fitting that the rose that bears his name should be, well, flamboyantly striped in scarlet and gold. It is happiest in a cool climate, the flowers opening rather quickly in hot weather.

Paul Barden

Helen Traubel

Hybrid tea, Herbert Swim/Armstrong Nurseries (USA), 1949.
Very large pink to apricot flowers, borne all season
on a tallish bush. Strong tea-rose scent.

Born in 1899 above her father's drugstore in St Louis, the singer Helen Traubel made her debut with the St Louis Symphony in 1923. In 1937 she joined New York's Metropolitan Opera, soon becoming its leading soprano and commanding enormous fees. She was at the height of her fame when this silken HT – one of the great American roses – was dedicated to her, but it's not just a rosy fan letter. She was a neighbour and close friend of Swim's boss Awdrey Armstrong, who broke his long-standing rule of not dedicating new roses to living people (how embarrassing if the rose bombed!) for her.

> . . . I know that for me,
> to whom flowers are part of desire,
> there are tears waiting
> in the petals of some rose.
>
> *Oscar Wilde*

Though celebrated for her Wagner, she was no musical snob and regularly sang in nightclubs and on radio and television – to the delight of her public but to the dismay of the Met management. Parting company with them in 1953, she diversified into Broadway musicals, cabaret, writing mystery novels, part-owning a baseball team, and displaying her talent for comedy on television and in several Hollywood movies. She died in 1972 after spending her last decade caring for her seriously ill husband.

Paul Barden

Helmut Schmidt

Hybrid tea, Reimer Kordes (Germany), 1979.
Large pure yellow flowers borne all season on a
tallish bush. Moderate tea fragrance.

The son of a Hamburg schoolmaster, Helmut Schmidt (1918–) studied economics, joined the Social Democratic Party, and was elected to the West German federal parliament in 1953. He served as minister for defence and of finance and as Chancellor from 1974 to 1982, in which role he worked both for German prosperity and for European unity. He retired from Parliament in 1986. Publisher of the influential magazine *Die Zeit* since 1983, Chancellor Schmidt remains one of Europe's most respected statesmen. He is also known as a promoter and patron of the arts, especially music – he is himself a talented pianist – and for his interest in conservation and the environment.

> We are all dreaming of some magical rose garden over the horizon instead of enjoying the roses that are blooming outside our windows today.
>
> *Dale Carnegie*

'Helmut Schmidt' has enjoyed a long career as one of the very best yellow HTs, but it's an old saying among rose-breeders that it's unwise to dedicate a rose to a politician; people who disagree with his policies are unlikely to buy it. It has been listed as 'Goldsmith' by some US and Canadian nurseries, and Kordes' British agent Mark Mattock also thought it advisable to rechristen it. So in Britain it is known as 'Simba' after Mr Mattock's golden Labrador dog!

Yvonne Arnold

Henri Martin

Moss, Jean Laffay (France), 1863.
Cherry-red, medium-sized flowers, sweetly scented and borne
in spring on a tallish bush. Bright red hips in autumn.

There aren't many red moss roses, and this one is generally acknowledged the best of them. Indeed it is sometimes called simply 'the Red Moss', but that is hardly fair to M. Martin.

Historian, member of the Académie Française, politician and writer of romantic novels, Henri Martin (1810–83) is best known in academic circles for his monumental *Histoire de France* (History of France), originally published in fifteen volumes between 1833 and 1836 and rewritten and expanded to sixteen volumes in 1861–65. But history may remember him better as a leader of the group of liberal intellectuals and artists who conceived the idea of creating the Statue of Liberty and presenting it to the United States as a silent but conspicuous protest against the dictatorial policies of the Emperor Napoléon III – who had already fallen from power by the time Auguste Bartholdi's *Liberty Enlightening the World* was finally installed in New York Harbour in 1883.

Don't confuse him with the minor Impressionist painter Henri Martin (1860–1943).

Dear rose, thy joy's undimmed,
Thy cup is ruby-rimmed,
Thy cup's heart nectar-brimmed.

Robert Browning

Paul Barden

Julia's Rose

Hybrid tea, Wisbech Plant Company (UK), 1976.
Shapely beige-tinted mauve flowers borne all season
on a fairly vigorous bush. Light fragrance.

'Julia' is Julia Clements (1906–), the 'high priestess of flower arrangement', as the British media called her. As well they might, for nobody has done more to popularise the art than she, through her lectures, her many books, and her organising of flower shows and flower arrangement societies. Her mission, as she called it, began one evening in 1947 at a meeting of a local Women's Institute. While waiting her turn to speak she noticed a bunch of flowers at the back of the hall and, throwing away her notes, she spoke instead of the joy that flowers could bring to the millions of women whose lives, like her own, had been torn apart by the war and of how the love of flowers might unite the people of the world in friendship.

> Go, lovely rose!
> Tell her that wastes her time and me
> That now she knows,
> When I resemble her to thee
> How sweet and fair she seems to be.
>
> *Edmund Waller*

A lifelong lover of the rose, she has had three dedicated to her: 'Julia Clements', (Wheatcroft, 1957), a red floribunda; 'Lady Seton', a scented warm pink HT (McGredy, 1964), named on the occasion of her marriage to Sir Alexander Seton; and 'Julia's Rose', adored by flower arrangers everywhere for its unique colour. It is at its best in spring and autumn.

Paul Barden

Just Joey

Hybrid tea, Roger Pawsey (Cants of Colchester, UK), 1972.
Large apricot flowers borne all season on a shortish
but vigorous bush. Excellent fragrance.

The colour of the elegantly ruffled flowers varies with the season, from peach to rich apricot, but it is always beautiful and distinctive – you could hardly mistake 'Just Joey' for any other rose. Voted 'world's favourite' by the World Federation of Rose Societies in 1994, it appreciates a little pampering.

The dedicatee is the wife of the raiser, Joanna Pawsey, known to her family and friends as Joey. In the old days her rose would have been 'Mrs Roger Pawsey', but that sort of formality is out of fashion, and somehow 'Joey Pawsey' didn't sound quite right for a rose.

'Why not just "Joey"?' his father suggested over breakfast one morning – and 'Just Joey' it became.

Mrs Pawsey loves to tell the story of how one day as she introduced herself to a customer the woman's face broke into a broad smile. 'Fancy that! I'm speaking to my favourite rose!'

Don't confuse her with Joseph Dunlop, OBE (1952–2000), the Irish motorcycle racing champion and humanitarian, who used to tell gushing fans he was 'just Joey'.

Flowers are beautiful hieroglyphics of nature,
with which she indicates how much she loves us.

Wolfgand von Goethe

Yvonne Arnold

Yvonne Arnold

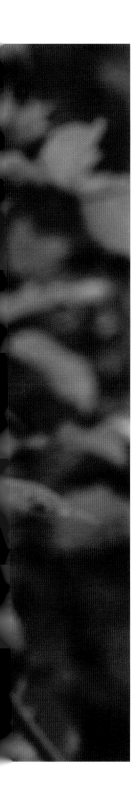

Katie Pianto's Rose

Rambler, origin unknown.
Smallish clear pink single flowers borne in sprays in late spring on a
vigorous climbing plant; orange hips follow. Light fruity scent.

This very pretty rose hangs over fences all around Australia and in New Zealand, but always anonymously, its owners having almost always acquired it as a cutting from a friend or neighbour. It is said that Katie Pianto, an Adelaide rose lover, fell in love with it on a visit to Sydney about forty years ago and took home a cutting. She was one of those grand rosarians who are the backbone of any rose society, who serve on all the committees and never miss a meeting or a show – and at every spring show she would display a bowl of this rose and offer cuttings to anyone who admired it.

Many accepted, for its beautiful fresh colour, long flowering season, clean shining foliage and pretty hips make it one of the most attractive ramblers; but nobody could identify it. When Katie died a few years ago in her mid-eighties there was a risk it might be lost, so the Adelaide rose growers Maureen and Andrew Ross decided to list it in their catalogue and to formally register the name by which all her friends knew it – 'Katie Pianto's Rose'.

La Belle Sultane

('Violacea') Gallica, raiser and date uncertain.
Medium-sized, almost-single violet-crimson flowers borne
in late spring on a tall bush. Sweet fragrance.

Most catalogues list this attractive rose as 'Violacea', but in his celebrated portraits of the roses grown by the Empress Joséphine at Malmaison, Pierre-Joseph Redouté gives it as 'La Belle Sultane', the beautiful Sultana.

> When love came first to earth,
> the Spring spread rose-beds to receive him.
>
> *Thomas Campbell*

Behind that name is a tale worthy of a grand opera. It is said that when Joséphine and her cousin the beautiful blonde and blue-eyed Aimée Dubucq de Rivéry were children in Martinique a blind seeress told their fortunes. Both would marry unhappily – but then they would become 'greater than Queens'. As we know, after a miserable first marriage to the Comte de Beauharnais, Joséphine went on to become Empress of the French; but in 1783 when Aimée was on her way to boarding school in France her ship was captured by Barbary pirates. They sold her to the Bey of Algiers, and he presented her to Sultan Abd-ul-Hamit I of Turkey for his harem at Topkapi. Aimée bore him a son, who became Sultan Mahmut II in 1808. He raised her to the rank of Sultana and for her sake reversed his predecessors' anti-French foreign policy. When she died in 1817, he inscribed her tombstone with the words 'her fame has made this country a paradise of roses'. A true story? Maybe.

Paul Barden

Lady Banks' Rose

Climber, introduced from China in the 19th century.
Clusters of small flowers in white or pale yellow smother
thornless evergreen plants in early spring.

Many an Australian gardener will tell you that the Banksian roses honour Sir Joseph Banks (1743–1820), the botanist who travelled with Captain Cook on his voyage to the South Seas. And they may imagine they are native to Australia. Not so! They come from China, whence the scented double white form (*R. banksiae alba-plena*) was introduced in 1807 by William Kerr, whom Sir Joseph, by then Director of Kew Gardens, had sent to the Orient to seek out new plants for the Kew collection.

Its name honours not Sir Joseph himself but his wife Dorothea (1758–1828), who ran the Banks estates in Lincolnshire while he was away botanising in foreign parts. When the new rose arrived Banks gave her a plant, which flowered before the one at Kew did. So it was given the name *R. banksiae* after her. It is often called the Lady Banks' Rose.

The double yellow (*R. banksiae lutea*) arrived in 1824. Both white and yellow are great favourites in mild-winter climates; but their daintiness of leaf and flower belies their immense vigour. The biggest rosebush in the world is a 120-year-old plant of the double white in a restaurant garden in Tombstone, Arizona.

Yvonne Arnold

Lady Hillingdon

Tea, Lowe & Sawyer (UK), 1910.
Large apricot-yellow to buff flowers borne all season on a tallish
bush or a moderately vigorous climber. Fine tea fragrance.

'Lady Hillingdon' appears to be the only rose credited to Lowe & Sawyer of Uxbridge near London, and it was perhaps natural for them to dedicate it to the local lady of the manor, Alice Lady Hillingdon (1857–1940) of Hillingdon Court. She was no doubt one of their best customers.

Charles William Mills, the second Baron Hillingdon (1855–1919) served his country with distinction both at home and abroad, though he never became Viceroy of India as some rose books claim. He married the Honourable Alice Harbord-Hamond in 1886. Lady Hillingdon enjoyed a reputation as an artist, but she is chiefly remembered today for the (almost certainly apocryphal) entry in her diary for the year 1912 in which she coined the phrase 'lie back and think of England'. They had one child, Arthur Robert, who duly became the third Baron, but the barony became extinct in 1982 and Hillingdon Court is now a school.

If you can resist giggling when you see it (I have a friend who can't), 'Climbing Lady Hillingdon' ranks among the most satisfactory of all climbing roses. The original bush version is excellent too.

> True friendship is like a rose:
> we don't realize its beauty until it fades.
>
> *Evelyn Loeb*

Paul Barden

Yvonne Arnold

Lady Mary Fitzwilliam

Hybrid tea, Henry Bennett (UK), 1882.
Light rose pink, large, shapely and very fragrant;
flowers all season but only moderately vigorous.

One of the most important names in rose history; almost every modern rose descends from 'Lady Mary Fitzwilliam', the first HT to be fully fertile. The lady herself was born in 1846, the daughter of the second Marquess of Ormonde, and in 1877 she married the Honourable William Fitzwilliam, son of the sixth Earl Fitzwilliam. Her Irish vivacity, wit and charm gave her entrée to royal circles (she was lady-in-waiting to the Duchess of Saxe-Coburg and a close friend of the Duchess of Edinburgh) and it is said that Bennett had to get the palace's permission to name the rose for her. No doubt it adorned her own garden at Wigganthorp House in Yorkshire, but despite its beauty and sweet fragrance most people found it difficult to grow. By the time she died in 1929 it had vanished from the catalogues.

Fearing it extinct, the great German raiser Wilhelm Kordes searched the world for it and in the early 1960s it was thought to have been found in New Zealand. Alas, that rose proved an impostor; but in 1975 a single plant was discovered in a garden in Norfolk, and this time it *was* the true 'Lady Mary'. Give it the best of everything and prune lightly.

> Footfalls echo in the memory,
> Down the passage which we did not take,
> Towards the door we never opened
> Into the rose garden.
>
> *T.S. Eliot*

Lamarque

Noisette, Maréchal (France), 1830.
Large lemon-white clustered flowers borne all year in mild
climates, on a very strong climbing plant. Sweet lemon scent.

If it hadn't been for the French Revolution and the subsequent wars, Jean Maximilien Lamarque (1770–1832) would probably have led a quiet life pursuing learning and culture on his family's estates in south-west France; but in 1793 he joined the army, in which he served with such distinction that Napoléon raised him to the rank of brigadier-general in 1801 and baron of the Empire in 1810. Upon Napoléon's return from Elba, he fought fiercely on his behalf and after Waterloo (1815) was exiled by King Charles X.

> Then will I raise aloft the milk-white rose,
> With whose sweet smell the air shall be perfumed.
>
> *Shakespeare*

Allowed to return in 1818, he entered parliament and was made count in 1828. His strong opposition to the anti-democratic policies of King Louis-Philippe made the old war hero a controversial figure but also a very popular one. He died in the cholera epidemic of 1832 and the anti-royalist party used his state funeral as a pretext to foment rebellion. Two days of bloody riots ensued, to be crushed with such brutality that some nurseries timidly rechristened the 'Lamarque' rose as 'Thé Maréchal' (Maréchal's Tea) after the rose-loving shoemaker who is said to have raised it from seeds sown in his window-box. It remains one of the all-time great roses.

Paul Barden

Lavender Pinocchio

Floribunda, Eugene Boerner (USA), 1948.
Café-au-lait and mauve flowers borne in sprays all
season on a bush of average height. Sweet scent.

Like 'Pink Peace' or 'Scarlet Queen Elizabeth', this is one of those bizarre names that arise when a raiser presents a new rose as a different-coloured version of some well-known variety. In this case the original 'Pinocchio' is pink – and 'Pinocchio' is not its original name.

Its raiser Wilhelm Kordes of Germany called it 'Rosenmärchen', the 'fairytale rose', but when Jackson & Perkins introduced it to America in 1940 they renamed it 'Pinocchio', after the fairytale character whose story had just been made into a hit movie by Walt Disney. The puppet who comes to life and whose punishment for telling a lie (having his nose grow longer) has become proverbial was not Disney's creation but that of the Italian author Carlo Collodi (1826–90), who published his tale in 1883 but never lived to see its fame.

'Pinocchio' was the leading floribunda of its day (it's still well worth growing), and J&P's hybridist Eugene Boerner bred a series of 'Pinocchios' – red, yellow, white, lavender – from its seed. 'Lavender Pinocchio' was the first mauve floribunda and in many ways is still the most satisfactory.

Yvonne Arnold

Lorraine Lee

Gigantea hybrid, Alister Clark (Australia), 1924.
Terra-cotta pink, medium-sized flowers borne virtually all year
on a vigorous climbing plant. Moderate scent.

This is the most famous rose ever raised in Australia, loved all over the country for its beautiful colour and ability to smother the house in roses even in winter. Its colour is so distinctive even now that raisers of other flowers have been known to describe them as 'Lorraine Lee' pink.

Sweet spring, full of sweet days and roses

George Herbert

Who was she, this lady with the melodious name? It turns out she was a cousin of Mrs Clark who, though Melbourne-born, had lived in England since her childhood and who had been awarded the MBE in 1918 for her work with the Women's Land Army during World War I. The rose was named to celebrate her trip to Australia in 1920 to visit her relatives, and it is said that when Clark discovered she was a keen rose lover he offered her the choice of any unnamed rose in his nursery beds. He was delighted when she picked the best – as well she might have, for gardening was in her blood. One of her great-uncles had been in charge of the gardens at Versailles in the days of Napoléon III.

That was the original bush version; the climbing sport that we all love didn't appear till 1932. Both need a warm climate to flower well.

Yvonne Arnold

Yvonne Arnold

Louis de Funès

Hybrid tea, Louisette Meilland, 1984.
Large high-centred flowers in orange and yellow, borne all
season on a strong bush. Mild fragrance.

Le Roi du Rire, the King of Laughter, the French call him, yet, despite his 127 films and many triumphs on the stage, Louis de Funès (1914–83) is almost unknown to English-speaking audiences. But though his career took off slowly – it was not until 1964 that *Le Gendarme de Saint-Tropez* (The Policeman of Saint-Tropez) made him famous – he remains one of the giants of French cinema, still drawing large audiences all over Europe.

In 1967 his wife, Jeanne, inherited from her aunt, the Comtesse de Maupassant, the beautiful seventeenth-century Château de Clermont on the north bank of the Loire near Nantes. There M. de Funès created one of the most beautiful rose gardens in Europe, conducted (like the estate's orchards and vineyards) entirely organically, with no sprays or chemical fertilisers. It is gone now, for after his death Mme de Funès had to sell the estate; but his movies are available on DVD and video, as funny as ever – and we have his rose, of which he was very proud. Exhibitors grizzle that the flowers open too quickly, but it is one of the first HTs to bloom in spring and the gaiety of its colours always gladdens the heart.

The Macartney Rose

Climber, introduced from China in 1794.
Medium-sized pure white single flowers borne in small clusters all season
on a very vigorous, evergreen plant. Pleasing lemon fragrance.

One of the more ludicrous episodes in the history of diplomacy is the 1793 British embassy to China. What with all the tea, silk and porcelain the British aristocracy had been buying, the balance of payments was heavily in China's favour, so His Majesty's government sent Lord George Macartney (1737–1806) to Peking to negotiate a more favourable trade agreement. He arrived in great state aboard a battleship and with an enormous retinue.

The Qianlong Emperor gave him an audience at the Summer Palace; but Chinese etiquette required ambassadors to kowtow before the emperor and Macartney refused to do anything more obsequious than to bow as he would before his own king. Qianlong was not impressed, and Macartney returned home virtually empty-handed — except for this rampant, viciously prickly but very beautiful rose. Gardeners called it the Macartney Rose, but the botanists preferred to call it *R. bracteata* after the unique nest of bracts in which each flower sits. (Don't confuse it with Meilland's 1995 pink HT 'The McCartney Rose', named after former Beatle Sir Paul McCartney.)

His failure in China didn't harm Lord Macartney's career: in 1796 he was made a baron and appointed Governor of South Africa.

Reign endless, Rose! for fair you are,
Nor Heaven reserves a fairer thing.

Herman Melville

Paul Barden

Maréchal Niel

Noisette, Henri Pradel (France), 1864.
Large butter-yellow flowers borne all season on a strong
but frost-tender climbing plant. Delicious tea scent.

Legend has it that one day a young general who had been unfairly passed over for promotion presented the first flowers of a new rose to the Empress Eugénie of France. Enchanted, she asked if it had a name.

'No, Madame,' said he.

'Then it shall be called the "Maréchal Niel", in honour of the gallant man who gave it to me.'

'Madame, I *am* honoured: but I am not a Marshal of France.'

'You are now!'

It's a charming story; but when Pradel dedicated his peerless yellow rose to him in 1864, Adolphe Niel (1802–69) was already a national hero: a member of the French Senate, holder of the Grand Cross of the Legion of Honour, and, yes, *Maréchal de France*, having been awarded the coveted baton at the Battle of Solferino in 1859. In 1867 he became Minister for War, but the bureaucracy frustrated his efforts to reform and modernise the French armed forces.

Happiest in mild-winter climates, 'Maréchal Niel' has long been popular in the American South – where some rose lovers will tell you that Mr Niel was a Texas marshall!

Paul Barden

Paul Barden

Margaret Merril

Floribunda, Harkness (UK), 1977.
Creamy-white, shapely flowers, borne in small long-stemmed
clusters on a bush of average height. Strong fragrance.

A sponsored rose, the sponsors in this case being the makers of the classic face lotion Oil of Ulan. With its beautiful faintly blushed complexion and its rose-water fragrance, the chosen rose was just right; but 'Oil of Ulan' would be a slightly odd name for a rose – even if the product weren't marketed under several names (Oil of Ulan, Olay or Ulay) in different countries. So it was decided to call the rose after the company's beauty adviser.

Perfect! Now to arrange a launch. Will the lady be able to be present to meet the press and the TV cameras? Er, um, actually she doesn't exist. Margaret Merril is just a nom-de-plume. Oh dear, but Jack Harkness had a happy thought. If any real-life Margaret Merril cared to introduce herself she would be given a bush of 'her' rose with the compliments of the raiser and the sponsors. Several have done so: and they have received an excellent rose, one of the most sweetly scented of all white roses. It may need protection from black spot.

> White ... is not a mere absence of colour;
> it is a shining
> and affirmative thing, as fierce as red,
> as definite as black ...
>
> *G.K. Chesterton*

Yvonne Arnold

Marjory Palmer

Floribunda, Alister Clark (Australia), 1936.
Deep pink, medium-sized flowers borne in clusters all
season on a shortish but strong bush. Sweet fragrance.

The raiser was a family friend of the Palmers of Dalvui Homestead, Noorat, Australia's foremost breeders of Romney Marsh sheep and whose garden was (and still is) one of the most celebrated in western Victoria. No doubt Marjory Palmer was delighted when he told her he was dedicating one of his very best roses to her – but (so her daughter wrote many years later) her rapture was a little modified when she discovered that it was deep rose pink, her least favourite colour! Still, she was too polite ever to say so in the raiser's hearing.

She would have had many people's sympathy. Nurserymen report that deep cool pink is the slowest-selling of all rose colours, the public preferring their pink roses to be softer and more delicate in tone or warmed with a touch of coral or apricot. But 'Marjory Palmer' remains an excellent rose, still one of the best floribundas of its colour, Australian-raised or otherwise. A lighter pink sport was registered in 1990 as 'Alister Clark'.

Maurice Utrillo

Hybrid tea, Arnaud Delbard (France), 2004.
Large flowers in red, striped with yellow and white,
borne all season on a tall bush. Good fragrance.

One of the best in a series of striped roses named for French Impressionist painters that Delbard call their 'Painters' Collection'. Henri Delbard relates that the idea came to him when he was admiring the fabulous collection of Impressionists in the Musée d'Orsay in Paris. And why not invite experts from the museum to actually name the roses so that each might in some way suggest its namesake's individual style? They were delighted to; and they were unanimous that this one should be named for Maurice Utrillo (1883–1955).

Die Rose ist ohne warum,
Sie blühet, weil sie blühet
(the rose has no reason why, she blooms, because she blooms)

Angelus Silesius

He was the illegitimate son of Suzanne Valadon (1865–1938), an artist's model who posed for every famous artist in Paris. Herself a talented painter, she was his only teacher and the streetscapes of Montmartre in Paris where they lived his chief subject. Recognition came slowly, but by 1920 he was universally recognised as a master and in 1929 he was awarded the Cross of the Legion of Honour. Despite his alcoholism, he painted till the day he died; and if you look closely at his pictures you'll see how he loved to juxtapose splashes of bright colour with white, just as on the petals of this rose.

Yvonne Arnold and Arnaud Delbard

139

Mme Caroline Testout

Hybrid tea, Joseph Pernet-Ducher (France), 1890.
Large, full-bodied rose-pink flowers on a sturdy, long-lived bush.
Excellent climbing sport. Mild fragrance.

Originally from Grenoble, Mme Testout was a *modiste* (they didn't call them 'fashion designers' back then) with a successful salon in Paris. The story goes that she was in Lyons buying silk when she learned that the town was also the centre of French rose-breeding. That gave her an idea – wouldn't a rose bearing her name be great publicity for her new London salon? So she introduced herself to the young M. Pernet-Ducher and offered him a suitable fee. Just how much he never revealed; but the satin-pink 'Mme Caroline Testout' made its debut at her salons the following spring.

> Vivez, si m'en croyez, n'attends à demain.
> Cueillez dès aujourd'hui les roses de la vie.
> (If you believe me, live! Don't wait for tomorrow.
> Gather the roses of life this very day.)
>
> *Pierre de Ronsard*

It was the best advertisement she ever had. Her creations are now a mere footnote in the history of fashion, but her rose seems immortal. Still widely admired in its own right (especially in its climbing form), it has been the parent and grandparent of many excellent roses. And when in 1904 the city of Portland, Oregon, decided that roses would look much nicer on its sidewalks than plain old grass, the first rose they planted – half a million bushes! – was 'Mme Caroline Testout'. Portland has been known as the City of Roses ever since.

Paul Barden

Mme Grégoire Staechelin

('Spanish Beauty') Climbing hybrid tea, Pedro Dot (Spain), 1927.
Large ruffled soft-pink flowers borne in spring on
a vigorous plant. Rich damask fragrance.

The lady was a friend of the raiser, and it is said Señor Dot dedicated this richly fragrant and much-admired rose to her as a wedding present. Her married name can be pronounced in several ways according to what part of Europe you come from; but we have it on the raiser's authority that she said *Shtahklin*, in the Swiss manner. And thereby hangs our tale. A Swiss friend once told me that when her uncle was a student at the University of Basel in the early 1930s, a certain Dr Grégoire Staechelin was professor of some dull medical speciality there. It seems his lectures were tedious indeed, but they were always crowded with students hoping for an invitation to lunch from his charming and very beautiful Spanish wife. If the story is true (and surely it must be!) then the rose's American name, 'Spanish Beauty', is a further tribute to her.

It is one of the first hybrid-tea type roses to bloom in spring, and while there is no repeat bloom it bears very handsome hips in autumn. The depth of colour varies with the season.

> And if you voz to see my roziz
> As is a boon to all men's noziz, –
> You'd fall upon your back and scream –
> 'Lawk! O criky! it's a dream!'

Edward Lear

Yvonne Arnold

Mme Hardy

Damask, Julien-Alexandre Hardy (France), 1832.
Snow-white, medium-sized flowers with a central green point borne in late
spring on a tall, rather lax bush. Fine rose-water fragrance.

This peerless rose was raised by Jean-Alexandre Hardy (1786–1876), formerly of the Empress Joséphine's garden at Malmaison but then Director of the botanic gardens of the Palais du Luxembourg in Paris, and named in honour of his wife, whose name we know from a different rose he dedicated to her in 1828 to have been Félicité.

It was said at the time that this one rose would make the raiser's name immortal. So it has turned out, though he raised several other roses still in the catalogues: the pear 'Beurre Hardy', and the remarkable red and yellow *Hulthemosa hardii*, a cross between a rose and a rare and intractable near-relative from Iran called *Hulthemia persica*.

> I think the true gardener is a lover of his flowers,
> not a critic of them
>
> *Reginald Farrer*

He was by all accounts a charming man, and a public servant of rare integrity as well. He refused to sell his new roses for personal gain, preferring to exchange propagating wood for new plants for the Luxembourg collection. It would seem entirely in character for him to call his masterpiece 'Mme Hardy' rather than giving it the more formal title 'Madame Alexandre Hardy'. We may read a happy, loving marriage into that.

Paul Barden

Paul Barden

Mme Isaac Pereire

Bourbon, Garçon (France), 1881.
Large quartered flowers in rich magenta-pink, borne all season
on a tall, rather leggy bush. Intense damask fragrance.

Rose books usually say only that this wonderfully fragrant rose honours the wife of a Parisian banker, but Isaac Rodriguez Pereire (1806–80) and his brother Jacob Emile (1800–75) built their vast fortune as developers and entrepreneurs; their banking was almost a sideline. They built railways (including France's first in 1832), property developments all over France (including Paris's ultra-fashionable Quartier Pereire), founded and ran a shipping line, and dabbled in politics and political journalism.

After his first wife's death, Isaac married Emile's daughter Fanny (1825–1910), the dedicatee of our rose. She was one of the great ladies of Parisian society, but after her husband's death spent most of her time at her country house, the Château Pereire at Gretz-Armanvilliers near Paris. In gratitude to the local surgeon who saved the life of her gravely ill child when the Paris doctors could do nothing, she built the hospital there; and in 1890 she lent Clement Ader (1841–1925) her park to try out his pioneering steam-powered aeroplane. It rose to the dizzy height of 15 centimetres and flew 50 metres before crashing.

I hear it is still a Pereire family tradition to plant a bed of 'Mme Isaac Pereire' in each of their gardens.

Mme Pierre Oger

Bourbon, Pierre Oger (France), 1878.
Shapely mid-sized flowers, palest pink blushing carmine, borne all
season on a slender, tallish bush. Excellent scent.

The dedicatee is the wife of the raiser, a nurseryman and market gardener from Caen in
Normandy. Pierre Oger (1816–94) is credited with raising fifteen new roses, all almost
forgotten today except for this one. It was not a seedling but a sport of 'La Reine Victoria',
an 1872 introduction from Joseph Schwartz of Lyon.

> Looking out on gardens and green things growing,
> The shadowy cups of roses flowering to themselves
>
> *A. L. Rowse*

It isn't often that a 'sported' rose becomes more popular than the parent from which it
sprang, but this one has: beside its delicate and beautiful colour the uniform rose-pink of
the otherwise identical 'La Reine Victoria' seems a trifle conventional. (Parent and daughter
do look lovely together both in the garden and the vase.) I doubt Queen Victoria would have
felt jealous of the nurseryman's wife. She was not really a keen gardener, and she had
several other roses named after her: 'Princess Victoria', a crimson gallica that has not come
down to us; the bright pink HP 'Souvenir de la Reine d'Angleterre' (Cochet, 1855), named
not posthumously but as a souvenir of her state visit to France that year; and the enormous
pink HP 'Her Majesty', introduced by Henry Bennett in 1885.

Yvonne Arnold

Montezuma

Hybrid tea ('grandiflora' in the US), Herbert Swim (USA), 1955.
Large shapely coral-rose flowers, borne all
season on a vigorous bush. Little scent.

When in 1955 Herb Swim presented Armstrong Nurseries with two new HTs in the then new hot-chilli tones, Mexican-themed names must have seemed just the thing: 'Aztec' and 'Montezuma'. The latter has proved much the better rose, and its name was an inspired choice. History remembers the Emperor Montezuma II (1466–1520) chiefly as the man who lost his empire and his life to a band of buccaneering Spaniards led by Hernán Cortéz; it is apt to forget that he was one of history's great gardeners. Even the conquering Spanish, for all their disapproval of the bloodthirsty Aztec religion, were obliged to admit that the royal gardens were more beautiful than any in Europe, and it is recorded that Montezuma himself sought out rare plants from all over his empire for their adornment.

> Roses grow on thorns and honey wears a sting.
>
> *Isaac Watts*

His rose is a worthy memorial. After a long period of eclipse by gaudier orange varieties, it has won many new admirers for its still unique colour and perfect form and for its great vigour, disease-resistance and freedom of bloom. It is a superb rose for cutting, but shelter it from the hot afternoon sun lest it scorch the flowers.

Yvonne Arnold

151

Rosa moyesii

Shrub, introduced from Sichuan in 1903.
Single blood-red flowers in spring on a very tall shrub.
Slight fragrance. Superlative scarlet hips in autumn.

The mountain country on the frontier of western China and Tibet where *R. moyesii* grows wild is hardly on the tourist routes even now; a century ago it was remote indeed. So when the botanist Ernest Wilson (1876–1930) came there in search of rare plants for the British nurserymen Veitch & Sons, it must have been a great comfort to him to find that in the market town of Tachienlu (Kanding) there was a station of the China Inland Mission – and that its superintendent, the Reverend James Moyes, was interested in botany. Moyes not only put Wilson and his team up at the Mission, he accompanied him on a plant-hunting trip across the border into Tibet.

Wilson dedicated *R. moyesii* to him by way of thanks; and Mr Moyes would have been delighted to hear that its wonderful flowers – the richest red of any wild rose – and its magnificent hips awoke Western gardeners to a new appreciation of the beauty of the wild roses. The clone known as 'Geranium' makes a less gawky shrub than the wild type. Give the plant a little shade from the hottest late-summer sun, which can scorch the ripening hips.

Yvonne Arnold

Mr Lincoln

Hybrid tea, Herbert Swim (USA), 1964.
Very large dark crimson, long-stemmed flowers borne all
season on a tall bush. Intense damask fragrance.

The dedication marks the centenary of the death of Abraham Lincoln (1809–65), perhaps the most widely revered president the United States has ever had. It is said he hated being addressed as President Lincoln, and in naming this superb red rose Herb Swim has honoured his wish that he be known simply as Mister Lincoln.

> We can complain because rose bushes have thorns,
> or rejoice because thorn bushes have roses.
>
> *Abraham Lincoln (paraphrasing Alphonse Karr)*

But there was another factor to be considered: back in Lincoln's own day there had been a rose called 'President Lincoln', and duplication of names is something the scrupulous raiser avoids. It is only a name in old books now, though the pleasing and fragrant cherry-red bourbon 'Souvenir du Président Lincoln' (Moreau & Robert, 1865) is still around. Mr Lincoln is also honoured by a fine dark red miniature rose with mossy buds raised by Jack Christensen in 1978 and bearing his nickname 'Honest Abe'.

Though mid-summer heat robs it of its rich colour, 'Mr Lincoln' is still the dark red rose of choice for many people, and not just patriotic Americans. Like all dark red roses it appreciates being pampered a little and may need protection against mildew.

Yvonne Arnold

Mrs B.R. Cant

Tea, Benjamin Cant (UK), 1901.
Large flowers varying from soft rose-pink to carmine and
borne all season on a spreading bush. Very good scent.

Founded in 1765, Cants of Colchester is the oldest firm of rose growers in the world, though it was not until about 1860 that the founder's grandson Benjamin Revett Cant decided to specialise exclusively in roses. He made his debut as a hybridist in 1875 with a crimson HP named 'Prince Arthur' after Queen Victoria's garden-loving son the Duke of Connaught, but it was not until 1901 that he felt he had raised a rose worthy to bear the name of his beloved Elizabeth, whom he had married in 1851 and who had borne him seven children. (And who, we may imagine, had presided over the tea and sandwiches at many a weekend cricket match when the Cant men under Ben's captaincy swept all before them.) Her patience was gloriously rewarded: to this day 'Mrs B.R. Cant' remains one of the most widely admired of all tea roses.

Ben's nephew Frank had set up on his own as a rose grower and breeder in 1878; but in 1967 their descendants merged the two rival firms of Benjamin R. Cant and Sons and Frank Cant and Sons. The present owners are Ben and Elizabeth's great-grandchildren Martin, Roger and Angela Pawsey.

It will never rain roses. When we want to have more roses,
we must plant more trees.

George Eliot

Yvonne Arnold

Mrs John Laing

Hybrid perpetual, Henry Bennett (UK), 1887.
Large cool pink flowers borne all season on a tall, almost
thornless plant. Beautiful damask fragrance.

Henry Bennett (1823–90) was one of the first rose breeders to pollinate his roses artificially (previous custom had been to simply plant the chosen parents together and trust the bees) and he proudly announced his roses as 'pedigree hybrids'. He gave most of them suitably blue-blooded names: 'Duchess of Connaught', 'Lady Mary Fitzwilliam', 'Her Majesty'; even the 'Honourable George Bancroft' was the American ambassador.

But not 'Mrs John Laing', which even in Bennett's day was regarded as the best of his creations – 'Beauty's queen' as one of the great Victorian rosarians called it. John Laing (1824–1901) was a leading London nurseryman, the raiser's agent in the capital. He was also a noted garden designer, laying out parks as far afield as Newcastle-upon-Tyne; and we may imagine his pleasure (and his wife's, for we may be sure she knew her roses too) when 'Mrs John Laing' turned out to be exceptional among the 'pedigree hybrids' in not being purely a show rose needing cosseting to produce a few perfect flowers. It was, and is, a first-rate rose in the garden, capable of giving as much pleasure as any pink rose raised in the century and a quarter since.

> People from a planet without flowers would think we must be mad
> with joy the whole time to have such things about us
>
> *Iris Murdoch*

Yvonne Arnold

Paul Barden

Mrs Sam McGredy

Hybrid tea, Sam McGredy III (UK), 1929.
Copper to salmon, shapely flowers borne all season on a
short bush or moderate climber. Light tea scent.

Samuel McGredy had founded the family nurseries at Portadown near Belfast in 1878, but it was his son, also named Sam (1861–1926), who first took up breeding roses. He had never put the family name on a rose, so it was quite an event when *his* son Sam III (1897–1934) decided to name one for his wife. He made a short list of candidates – and Ruth McGredy would have none of them, choosing instead a rose Sam wasn't even planning to introduce.

She was right, too! 'Mrs Sam McGredy' not only became one of the favourite roses of the 1930s, it is the rose the McGredy family chose in 1958 to adorn their coat of arms. With its unique coppery colour and the splendid mahogany tint of its young leaves, 'Mrs Sam' remains a classic, never mind that the full-blown flower quickly fades to salmon-pink or that the bush isn't very strong. (The climbing version is much easier to grow.) Perhaps Sam was hoping that further breeding would correct those faults, but it was not to be. He died young, and it was not till his son, Sam IV, came of age in the 1950s that the long parade of fine McGredy roses resumed.

It's a good thing no rose is perfect,
or we rose breeders would be out of a job.

William Kordes

Octavius Weld

Tea, date and raiser unknown.
Large cream and blush flowers borne all season on a
tallish, spreading bush. Good tea fragrance.

'Found roses', they are called – roses that old-rose enthusiasts have discovered in old gardens, parks and cemeteries and saved for posterity by propagating and introducing them. Of course they are rarely found with their names attached, so their discoverers give them 'provisional' ones. Here is a fine Australian example, discovered at Blakiston Cemetery near Adelaide a few years ago and given the name visible among the lichens on the nearest headstone – 'Octavius Weld'.

> Dich lieb' ich wie die Rose ihren Strauch …
> (I love you as the rose loves its rosebush …)
>
> *Friedrich Rückert*

It turns out to have been a happy choice. Born in England, Dr Octavus (not Octavius!) Weld gained his MD from New York University in 1859, took up the post of ship's doctor on the *Irene*, and arrived in the colony of South Australia in 1860. He set up his practice in the Adelaide Hills town of Nairne (the first doctor to do so) and married a local girl, Ann Johnstone. In 1871 the Welds moved to nearby Mt Barker, whose doctor he was till his death in 1901. He would surely have been delighted with his rose, as he was a keen gardener and for some years served as president of the Floricultural Society of South Australia.

Yvonne Arnold

Omar Khayyam

Damask, Graham Thomas (UK), c.1950.
Medium-sized rose-pink flowers borne in small sprays in
spring on a fairly compact bush. Superb fragrance.

In his own country Omar Khayyam (c.1050–c.1122) is remembered as much as a mathematician and astronomer as a poet, but thanks to the translation by Edward Fitzgerald (1809–93) of his *Rubaiyat* (Quatrains) he is by far the best known Persian poet in the West.

Published in 1859, the *Rubaiyat* was an immediate hit, and in about 1890 some students from Cambridge University made a pilgrimage to Omar's tomb at Nashipur. He is said to have asked that his grave should be 'where the north wind will scatter rose petals over it', and indeed a rosebush still grew there. It wasn't in flower, but they were able to bring home a hip or two and sow the seeds. In 1893 they planted one of the seedlings on Fitzgerald's grave in the churchyard of Boulge in Suffolk.

It is that rose which Graham Thomas propagated many years later and introduced as 'Omar Khayyam'. It is a pretty rose, beautifully scented, and a living link to the old poet who so loved wine and roses.

Each morn a thousand roses brings, you say;
Yes, but where leaves the rose of yesterday?

Omar Khayyam

Yvonne Arnold

Papa Meilland

Alain Meilland (France), 1963.
Large deep-red flowers borne all season on a bush of average
height. Superlative fragrance, but watch for mildew.

'We knew this rose as Caesar during its trials, but my old friend Antoine Meilland
– reluctantly, for he is very modest – consented to my suggestion that his name be put
upon it.'

So Meilland's British agent Harry Wheatcroft tells us; and it is said that, when he
pointed out how fitting it would be for the finest Meilland rose since 'Mme Antoine Meilland'
('Peace') to bear Antoine's name, the family at once joined him in twisting their dear Papa's
arm.

A rose, as red as a shaded lantern.

Sa'adi

The son of a market gardener, Antoine Meilland (1884–1971) fell in love with the rose
when still a schoolboy. At sixteen he went to work for the Lyon rose grower and breeder
Francis Dubreuil, and in 1909 married his boss's daughter, Claudia. It was their son Francis
(1912–58) who raised the Meilland firm from just another successful family-run rose
nursery to one of the world's leading creators of new roses; but by 1963 Papa was the doyen
of French rose growers. Wheatcroft had little joy from 'Papa Meilland' in Britain, where it
mildews badly; but in sunny climates it is a glorious rival to its parent 'Charles Mallerin'.
The World Federation of Rose Societies voted it 'world's favourite rose' in 1988.

Yvonne Arnold

Paul Barden

Paul Neyron

Hybrid perpetual, Antoine Levet (France), 1869.
Huge rose-pink flowers borne all season on a tall, almost
thornless bush. Sweet but variable fragrance.

Until 'Peace' came along, 'Paul Neyron' reigned virtually unchallenged as the largest of all roses. Huge size and a multiplicity of petals can of course be merely vulgar, but not in this case; the friend of mine who spoke of its 'heroic beauty' put it well. It is a rose worthy of a hero.

Paul Neyron was such a one: a friend of the raiser, a medical student who distinguished himself by courageously tending the sick and wounded during the disturbances (as history calls them) of the Commune and lost his life during the siege of Paris. He was only twenty-three.

> Sur tout parfum, j'aime la rose.
> (Above all perfumes, I love the rose.)
>
> *Pierre de Ronsard*

So rose books inform us – but the historian might quibble that the bloody siege in which the government forces crushed the rebellious Paris Communards took place in 1871 and the rose is dated 1869. Still, M. Levet surely knew his young friend well, and who is to say that he did not discern in him the signs of future greatness? Like all HPs, 'Paul Neyron' needs generous cultivation to show its full magnificence. Its distinctive and beautiful colour has passed into gardeners' lexicon as 'neyron rose'.

Peace

('Mme A. Meilland', 'Gioia', 'Gloria Dei') Hybrid tea,
Francis Meilland (France), 1942. Very large yellow flowers blushed pink,
borne all season on a strong, glossy-leaved bush. Mild fragrance.

The story has often been told of how the young Francis Meilland had this wonderful rose, his masterpiece, almost ready for introduction when war descended on the world; of how his American agent Robert Pyle received the precious propagating wood in the diplomatic bag; of how he announced it to the world as 'Peace', on the very day Berlin fell to the Allies.

Cut off by the war, Pyle didn't know that Meilland had already named the rose 'Mme Antoine Meilland' in memory of his mother, who had died in 1932 in her early 40s. This was no conventional tribute. Claudia Meilland was the daughter of a rose breeder, Francis Dubreuil; so when the teenaged Francis suggested the family firm should go into the financially risky business of breeding she gave him her full support and passed on the knowledge she had learned at her father's knee. She watched over him as he pollinated his flowers and sowed his seeds; she comforted him when his puppy dug up his first seedlings and as he judged his new roses her trained eye assisted his . . .

The 'Peace' rose has become a universal symbol of hope; but Francis was right to remember Claudia. Without her it might never have been born.

It humbles me to know that when people around the world see my rose they shout for joy, give glory to God and most earnestly desire peace.

Francis Meilland on the 'Peace' rose

Yvonne Arnold

Yvonne Arnold

Picasso

Floribunda, Sam McGredy IV (UK), 1971.
Small flowers blending red, pink and white and borne
in large sprays all season on a compact bush. Faint scent.

Pablo Picasso (1881–1973) very rarely painted roses, but that hardly detracts from his status as the twentieth century's greatest, most versatile and innovative artist. He is said to have wished to be known as one of its great lovers too, but this is not the place to talk of that.

His rose was the first of what Sam McGredy called his 'hand painted' strain, which is distinguished by the way two shades of red or pink are blotched and marbled together on each petal around a white or pale yellow centre. Most raisers give their promising seedlings nicknames while they are on trial and Sam has written that while the strain was being developed he gave them Spanish names like José and Pepé. When the time came to formally name the first an artist was the obvious choice, and who better than the great Spanish master? He happily accepted the honour, but he's a hard act to follow and subsequent roses in the series were not named for artists. The 'hand painted' effect is more striking in some seasons than others, but 'Picasso' always puts on an eye-catching show.

Pierre de Ronsard

Modern climber, Marie-Louise Meilland (France), 1987.
Large soft-pink flowers, borne all season on a
moderately vigorous climber. Mild fragrance.

Meilland was a little late in marking the 400th anniversary of the death of the Prince of
Poets, but that hardly matters; this is a very fine rose and deservedly a great favourite.

Youngest son of a high official at the court of Francis I, Pierre de Ronsard (1524–85)
was destined for a career as a diplomat; but when he became deaf at the age of seventeen
he retired to devote himself to study and poetry. Rejecting the elaborately artificial style
then in vogue, he sought a simpler one more in harmony with the natural rhythms of the
French language and his love poems, especially, were admired all over Europe. Charles IX
of France, Elizabeth I of England and Mary Queen of Scots were among his patrons; but
after his death fashions changed and his works went out of print. It was only in the early
nineteenth century that the Romantics rediscovered him and restored him to his rightful
place in European literature.

He was an ardent lover of the rose, whose beauty he sang in poem after exquisite poem.
How then could Meilland have allowed his rose to be sold in America under the fatuous
name 'Eden Climber'?

Prends cette rose aimable comme toi,
Qui sert de rose aux roses les plus belles
(Take this rose, as lovely as you are,
Which makes the most beautiful roses blush)

Pierre de Ronsard

Yvonne Arnold

Président de Sèze

Gallica, Mme Hébert (France), 1828.
Medium-sized flowers blending shades of pink, mauve and violet,
borne in spring on an upright bush. Sweet fragrance.

This is the tale of two fine roses, 'Président de Sèze' and 'Jenny Duval'. Old books sometimes list 'Président de Sèze' as 'Mme Hébert' after its raiser, whose husband Michel Hébert was a lawyer in Rouen. Which might explain the dedication to Comte Romain de Sèze (1748–1828), who was a very prominent lawyer indeed. Originally from Bordeaux, he became President of the Court of Appeals and defended Louis XVI at his trial by the Revolutionaries in 1792.

'Jenny Duval' is usually credited to one Charles Duval, c. 1840. Jenny was most likely his wife or daughter, though it has been suggested that she might be the actress Jeanne Duval, 'the black Venus' celebrated in the poems of her lover Charles Baudelaire (1821–67), or maybe a (fictitious) Louisiana girl who features in a song popular during the American Civil War.

Paul Barden's picture is of 'Jenny Duval' – 'Président de Sèze' usually shows a much deeper centre and an almost-white rim. But the American Rose Society, the authority in such matters, has decreed that they are the same variety and must be called 'Président de Sèze'. The moral might be that young ladies should beware of sharp lawyers!

> Rose is a rose is a rose is a rose
>
> *Gertrude Stein*

Paul Barden

Yvonne Arnold

Princess of Wales

Floribunda, Jack Harkness (UK), 1997.
Medium-sized ivory-white blooms, borne in clusters all
season on a short-growing bush. Very mild fragrance.

Princess Diana loved white flowers, so it was no surprise that when in April 1997 she consented to lend her name to a rose she chose the white floribunda from the five candidates submitted by the raisers. 'Princess of Wales' was unveiled on her birthday that summer at the Hampton Court flower show, with the news that she had instructed that a portion of its profits be given to charity. (In Australia, it benefits the Victor Chang Cardiac Research Institute.)

Only a few weeks later she was dead, and the world wept over the bouquet of 'Princess of Wales' roses her sons placed on her coffin. Surely this was the saddest debut any new rose has ever made, and it is to the Harkness firm's credit that they have never exploited it in their publicity. But is the rose worthy of her? Yes, it is: many rosarians rate it the finest white rose of the last forty years.

Other roses dedicated to her (all posthumously) include the pink and cream exhibition HT 'Diana, Princess of Wales' from Jackson & Perkins; David Austin's palest peach 'England's Rose'; Gareth Fryer's pink HT 'Princess Charming'; and Frank Cowlishaw's purple 'Forever Royal'.

Princesse de Monaco

Hybrid tea, Alain Meilland (France), 1981.
Very large pink-edged cream flowers borne all season
on a bush of average height. Moderate fragrance.

It was a storybook romance. The Philadelphia-born actress Grace Kelly (1929–82) had come to Monaco to star in Alfred Hitchcock's movie *To Catch a Thief*, which was being shot on location there. She met Monaco's Sovereign Prince, the dashing Rainier III (1923–2005). They fell in love, and in April 1956 they married.

Francis Meilland celebrated the occasion with the rose-pink, richly fragrant hybrid tea 'Grace de Monaco' – the most precious of all her wedding presents, the garden-loving Princess Grace once remarked. A large bed was planted in front of the palace in Monte Carlo; but by 1981, when Monaco was to host an international rose conference, the bushes were getting tired and Meilland was unable to supply sufficient replacements.

> When at last I took the time to look into the heart
> of a flower, it opened up a whole new world
>
> *Princess Grace of Monaco*

What to do? Francis' widow Louisette solved the problem. At the Monte Carlo flower show the princess had fallen in love with a shapely new HT whose colours suggested those of Monaco's red and white flag; and though Meilland had originally intended to call it 'Preference', Louisette christened it 'Princesse de Monaco'.

It is a very beautiful rose and a bestseller, but don't overlook 'Grace de Monaco', which remains a fine rose.

Yvonne Arnold

Queen Elizabeth

Floribunda ('grandiflora' in the US). Walter Lammerts (USA), 1954.
Large candy-pink flowers, borne singly and in small clusters
all season on a very tall bush. Slight fragrance.

That Dr Lammerts had sought and obtained the British Embassy's permission for the name didn't stop more than one prominent British rosarian grumbling when 'Queen Elizabeth' came out that it was 'a pity that an *American* rose should be so called'. They were a minority, however; most British rose lovers rejoiced that their new Queen should be honoured by such a superlative rose. (It remains one of the world's favourite roses, its only demerit being the faintness of its scent.) We may be sure Her Majesty was delighted too. She is a keen rosarian – indeed, a friend in charge of an historic garden she was to open some years ago was asked by her staff not to encourage her to talk roses or they'd never get her to her next appointment on time!

Several roses have been dedicated to her: 'Princess Elizabeth' (Wheatcroft, 1927), a yellow-and-red hybrid tea; 'Lilibet' (Lindquist, 1953), a pale pink floribunda; 'The Queen' (Lowe, 1954), an indifferent orange-blend HT; the bizarrely named but excellent 'Scarlet Queen Elizabeth' (Dickson, 1963), a big-growing orange-red floribunda; and the outstanding HT 'Silver Jubilee' (Cocker, 1977), which the late Queen Mother once described as a confection in pink.

Paul Barden

183

Rosa Mundi

(R. gallica versicolor) Gallica, early seventeenth century.
Medium-sized flowers striped in cerise and blush-white,
borne in late spring on a compact bush. Sweet scent.

Oldest of all striped roses – and still one of the most beautiful – 'Rosa Mundi' supposedly honours a lady known as the Fair Rosamond. Legend has it that to guard her virtue from the lecherous King Henry II, her father had sent her to live with the nuns at Godstow Abbey near Oxford; but Henry contrived to meet her by telling the abbess that he had come to see her roses. He and Rosamond became lovers, and after his marriage to Eleanor of Aquitaine he installed her in a secret house hidden in a maze of roses (all 'Rosa Mundi', of course!) in the grounds of the Palace of Woodstock; but the jealous Eleanor found her way in and poisoned her . . .

Or so the balladeers sang – but the lady's real name was Jane Clifford, and while she was indeed King Henry's mistress, she ended the relationship soon after his marriage and became a nun at Godstow, where she died of natural causes in 1176. 'Rosa Mundi' only appeared some 450 years later, as a sport of the plain red *R. gallica officinalis* in a garden in Norfolk – and its name means simply 'the worldly or sophisticated rose', which a striped rose certainly is.

Rose of all Roses, Rose of all the World!

William Butler Yeats

Paul Barden

Satchmo

Floribunda, Sam McGredy IV (UK), 1970.
Orange-red, medium-sized flowers borne in clusters all season
on a bushy plant of average height. Faint scent.

Lovers of jazz will recognise the dedicatee of this rose as Louis Armstrong (1898–1971), the great trumpeter and singer. He first learned to play the cornet as a child in a New Orleans orphanage, and it is said that his classmates there first gave him the nickname Satchmo, which is short for 'satchel-mouth', from his unusual embouchure.

Sam McGredy has said that the dedicatees of new roses almost always expect to be given free plants, often several dozen of them; but when he wrote to Mr Armstrong asking if a lifelong fan might have the pleasure of dedicating a rose to him, the old maestro replied that he would be honoured; but could he ask a favour in return? Might he have a plant, just one, to grow in his garden in Hoboken?

Of course; and when in 1977 Sam raised a new scarlet floribunda that he considered an improvement on 'Satchmo' (its colour is brighter), he named it 'Trumpeter', in the great man's memory.

> I see trees of green, red roses too
> I see them bloom, for me and you
> And I think to myself, what a wonderful world!
>
> *Sung by Louis Armstrong*

Yvonne Arnold

Paul Barden

Sombreuil

('Mlle de Sombreuil') Climbing tea,
Robert (France), 1851. Large ivory-white flowers borne
all season on a strong climbing plant. Intense fragrance.

It is 2 September 1792 and France is in the grip of the Reign of Terror. A mob breaks into the Prison de l'Abbaye and starts butchering the aristocrats being held there. But when they come to the aged Marquis de Sombreuil, Charles Virot (1727–94) and his daughter Marie (1774–1823), they hesitate. He is an old soldier, and she is so young and beautiful. A man in the crowd seizes the moment. In exchange for her father's life, Marie must renounce her aristocracy and seal her vow by drinking an aristocrat's blood. He hands her a goblet. She drinks; the mob cheers; the massacre ceases.

> O gather me the rose, the rose,
> While yet in flower we find it,
> For summer smiles, but summer goes,
> And winter waits behind it.
>
> *William Ernest Henley*

So Jules Michelet relates in his *Histoire de la Révolution Française*, published in 1847; and with the story fresh in everyone's mind, M. Robert dedicated 'Mlle de Sombreuil' to the young heroine's memory. Alas, her father was guillotined anyway in 1794 and, having fled France, Marie returned after the Revolution a widow and died in poverty. And the rose we know by her name today is not Robert's original. What it might be is uncertain; but it is a superb rose, well worthy of her name.

Paul Barden

Souvenir de la Malmaison

Bourbon, Jean Béluze (France), 1842.
Large palest-pink flowers borne freely all season on a
medium-height bush or strong climber. Excellent fragrance.

Legend has it that on a visit to the raiser's nursery the Grand Duke Michael of Russia was invited to name this new rose, and that it was he who chose the romantic name 'Souvenir de la Malmaison' in memory of the Empress Joséphine, with whom as a young man he had been in love. (She refused him, saying Russia would be too cold for her.)

Well, maybe; but it was an inspired choice, for few houses are more closely identified with their chatelaine than the Château de Malmaison, whose odd name (the house of evil or of sickness) comes from it having served as a leper hospital in the fifteenth century. The newly wed Napoléon and Joséphine had bought it in 1799, and it was there among her roses that she spent the happiest years of her marriage; it was there that she spent her last sad days as the divorced wife of a fallen Emperor; and it was there, on 29 May 1814, that she died. She's buried not in Paris but in the local parish church.

Whether in its original bush version or the climbing sport (said to have originated in Australia about 1890), the rose is a splendid tribute to her. The nineteenth-century rosarians who called it 'the queen of beauty and fragrance' spoke the truth.

Souvenir d'un Ami

Tea, Bélot-Défougère (France), 1846.
Large warm-pink flowers borne all season on a tallish,
spreading bush. Very sweet fragrance.

'In memory of a friend.'

This must be the most poignant of all rose names, and ever since 'Souvenir d'un Ami' came out people have asked whom it honours and what happened. We may never know. All M. Bélot-Défougère has told us is that he did not raise the rose, it was raised and named by an amateur who swore him to secrecy.

Tis better to buy a small bouquet
And give to your friend this very day,
Than a bushel of roses white and red
To lay on his coffin after he's dead.

Irish Proverb

Still, the very lack of particulars makes the sentiment universal, and that makes this rose an excellent choice if you want to plant a rosebush as a memorial. Like the friend in California who, unable to find a rose whose name bore any resemblance to her late husband's, chose this one to plant on his grave. It is a good choice in another way too – roses in public places rarely get the day-to-day attention that those in private gardens do, and like many of the teas 'Souvenir d'un Ami' needs little pruning or other care and flowers virtually all year in mild-winter climates. (In frosty ones it appreciates a warm, sheltered position.) And the gently nodding flowers are so beautiful in their tender colour and sweet fragrance.

Yvonne Arnold

Yvonne Arnold

Sutter's Gold

Hybrid tea, Herbert Swim (USA), 1949.
Large flowers in yellow touched with red, borne all season
on a tall bush. Excellent tea-rose fragrance.

'McGredy's Yellow', 'Verschuren's Pink', 'Paul's Scarlet' – most such roses bear the names of their raisers, but Johann Augustus Sutter (1803–80) was no rose breeder. Of Swiss descent, he emigrated to America to make his fortune, eventually settling in California where in 1840 he took up a grant of 20,000 hectares of land near where the city of Sacramento now stands. He called it 'New Switzerland', intending to develop it as an agricultural utopia. But in 1848 gold was discovered in a creek on his property. The news got out and the great Gold Rush of 1849 was on; and the diggers, supported by the US Supreme Court, effectively forced Sutter off his own land. He spent the rest of his life seeking compensation from the government and died in poverty.

In 1925, the Swiss novelist Blaise Cendrars (1887–1961) published a romanticised account of Sutter's life which was filmed by Universal Studios in 1936. Both book and movie were called *Sutter's Gold* – so when Armstrong Nurseries marked the centenary of the gold rush with this classic rose, 'Sutter's Gold' was the obvious name. Often the first HT in bloom in spring, it is one of the strongest-scented of all yellow roses.

Tiffany

Hybrid tea, Robert Lindquist (USA), 1954.
Large flowers in warm pink with a touch of yellow,
borne all season on a very upright bush. Intense fragrance.

Founded in 1837, Tiffany & Co. of Fifth Avenue is perhaps the world's most famous jewellers, but the man who made their name a household word is not remembered for his work with diamonds. He was Louis Comfort Tiffany (1848–1933), the son of the founder, and he is famous for his iridescent glass. His studio made it into vases and jugs and goblets, into stained-glass windows for both church and living room, and above all into the Tiffany lamps featuring flowers like water-lilies, wisteria and, of course, roses. Cheap imitations abound, signed originals fetch fabulous prices. He was an interior designer too, and in 1881 redecorated the state apartments of the White House for President Chester Arthur.

> I'd rather have roses on my table
> than diamonds around my neck.
>
> *Emma Goldman*

Whether Mr Lindquist intended to dedicate this classic rose to Tiffany's memory he didn't say; but by the 1950s 'Tiffany' had become a byword for something precious and beautiful. It has become popular as a girl's name, at least in the US, and as such it is a suitable name for a rose which after half a century remains a favourite for its elegant form, lovely colour and sweet fragrance.

Yvonne Arnold

Yvonne Arnold

Tipsy Imperial Concubine

Tea, introduced from China by Hazel le Rougetel in 1989.
Shapely pink and cream flowers, borne all season on a
tallish bush. Excellent fragrance.

The lady's real name was Yang Guifei. Born in 712 AD, she was the most beautiful woman in China. The Tang dynasty was then at the height of its glory; and on the throne was the highly cultivated Emperor Xuanzong, known as Ming-huang, the Radiant Golden Emperor. Already an old man when Guifei entered his household, he was besotted with her. Anything she wanted – and her extravagance was legendary – he gave her, even grape wine imported from Persia. (The court snickered and called her 'the tipsy concubine'.) Nor did he object to her passionate affair with a handsome young general called An Lushan.

But in 755 An Lushan rose in bloody rebellion, forcing the government to flee to distant Sichuan. Whether Guifei was involved is uncertain even now; but the commander of the Imperial troops intercepted a letter and the Emperor was forced to execute her for treason. It is said he died of a broken heart. In 757 An Lushan was murdered by his own son and the civil war ended; but the country never really recovered, and in 907 the Tang fell.

A Chinese Jezebel or a tragic, romantic heroine? Smell her rose and decide for yourself. It dislikes wet weather.

Rosa wichurana variegata

Rambler or ground cover, origin unknown.
Small scented white flowers in sprays in summer on an
evergreen, trailing plant with variegated leaves.

This rather rare rose has the distinction of being one of only three to have variegated leaves, the others being Delbard's brand-new red floribunda 'Elie Semoun' and a black-spot prone red and yellow HT called 'Curiosity' (Cocker, 1971). *R. wichurana variegata* is healthy and almost evergreen; and while it isn't always very vigorous or free with its flowers it is a very pretty plant. Few flower arrangers can resist its pink-tinted young shoots and little white-splashed leaves.

Max Ernst Wichura (1817–66) was a junior magistrate in Breslau in Prussia, but he was also a distinguished botanist. Charles Darwin quoted his studies of hybrid willows in *The Origin of Species*, and in 1859 the Prussian government invited him to join its scientific expedition to the Orient. (What the bureaucrats in Berlin thought of his habit of garnishing his plant drawings with caricatures is not recorded.) It was in Japan that he collected the species that has made his name familiar to rose lovers. Not introduced to the West until after his death, *R. wichurana* has been the parent of many fine climbing roses (among them 'Albertine', 'Dr Van Fleet' and 'Dorothy Perkins') and through its hybrid, *R. × kordesii*, an ancestor of many fine recent roses of all types.

Paul Barden

202

William Lobb

Moss, Jean Laffay (France), 1855.
Darkly mossy buds and mid-sized purple and mauve flowers,
borne in spring on a rather gangly bush. Very sweet fragrance.

Though it has always been criticised for its lanky growth (give it a stake or two or train it over the lower limbs of a climber such as 'Albertine'), this is one of the classic purple Victorian roses, and its dedicatee is one of the great Victorian horticulturists. Not that William Lobb (1809–63) would have seen his rose very often – he spent most of his career travelling in the wilder parts of the two Americas collecting rare plants to send back to England to his employers, the great British nursery firm of Veitch & Sons of Exeter. (His younger brother Thomas collected orchids for them in South-East Asia.)

William Lobb introduced many fine shrubs and flowers, but his fame rests on the two great conifers without which no Victorian or Edwardian garden with any claim to grandeur was complete – the monkey puzzle tree (*Araucaria araucana*), sent back from Chile in 1842, and the newly discovered wellingtonia or giant sequoia (*Sequoiadendron giganteum*) of California, which he took back to England in 1852. After his retirement in 1858 he settled in San Francisco, where he spent the rest of his life. Alas, no portrait of him appears to survive.

William Shakespeare

Shrub, David Austin (UK), 1987 and 2000.
Large flowers in crimson fading to purple, borne all
season on a tallish bush. Strong damask fragrance.

David Austin calls his modern roses with Victorian-style flowers his 'English Roses', and among the famous Englishmen and women for which many are named are several Shakespearean characters. But he has written that only a superlative red rose could be worthy of Shakespeare himself, whose love of the rose is attested by the many times it appears in his poems and dramas.

> Their lips were four red roses on a stalk,
> Which in their summer beauty kiss'd each other.

Shakespeare

He waited for a quarter of a century for such a rose, and in 1987 it appeared: 'William Shakespeare'. It was, and is, a fine rose; but in 2000 Mr Austin brought out an improved version which he called 'William Shakespeare 2000'. (Very similar in its flowers, it is said to score over the original in being healthier and freer-blooming.) His explanation for its rather extraordinary name is that a poll conducted by a British newspaper that year awarded Mr Shakespeare (1564–1616) the title of 'Englishman of the millennium' – but many Australian nurseries prefer to call it 'New William Shakespeare'.

Some prefer the 1987 'William Shakespeare', others the new one. The choice is yours, but check the codename. The original is AUSroyal, the new is AUSromeo.

Paul Barden

Yolande d'Aragon

Hybrid perpetual, Jean Vibert (France), 1843.
Large flowers in rose pink tinted mauve, borne all season
on a fairly tall bush. Strong damask fragrance.

Though not exactly famous today, the beautiful Yolande (Iolanthe) of Aragon (1379–1442) played an important role in the tangled politics of France during the second phase of the Hundred Years' War. The daughter of King John I of Aragon, she married Louis II, Duke of Anjou and King of the Two Sicilies, in 1400. When in 1422 the Dauphin Charles de Valois (1403–61) married her daughter Marie, she invited him to live at her court in Saumur, thus keeping him out of the treacherous clutches of the pro-English faction at the court in Paris. An early and strong supporter of Joan of Arc, she financed Joan's army at the decisive siege of Orléans in 1429 that cleared the way to the Dauphin's triumphant coronation as Charles VII in Reims Cathedral later that year. For the rest of her life she remained one of Charles's most trusted advisers.

Issued on the 400th anniversary of her death, Vibert's superbly fragrant rose has only been restored to the catalogues fairly recently, but already it features prominently in many lists of favourite old roses. It is bushier in growth and more continuous in bloom than most HPs.

The lady's portrait is taken from a stained-glass window in Le Mans Cathedral.

Yvonne Arnold

Yvonne Arnold

Zéphirine Drouhin

Bourbon, Bizot (France), 1868.
Deep pink, mid-sized flowers borne in small clusters
in spring and autumn on a thornless climbing plant. Delicious scent.

Its freedom from prickles – it has always been nicknamed The Thornless Rose – its great freedom of bloom, its beautiful colour and above all its wonderful scent have made 'Zéphirine Drouhin' a great favourite for 140 years. It is dedicated, so the raiser has told us, to 'Mme Zéphirine Drouhin, the wife of a horticulturist resident in Semur in the Côte d'Or'.

'A local girl!' exclaimed a rose-loving friend who has a house in the pretty hilltop town, the full name of which is Semur-en-Auxois. Might she still have descendants there? Apparently not; my friend found no Drouhins in the local phone book. The Côte d'Or is home to Burgundy's greatest wines, and one of the leading names in the trade is the old firm of Joseph Drouhin et Cie, founded in 1882. But enquiries there also led nowhere.

So it seems that we may never learn any more about the lady than that she was a rose lover. But do we really need to know more than that? After all, is there any higher qualification for the honour of lending one's name to a rose than that of loving roses?

BEAUTIFUL
ROSES
FOR ...

Yvonne Arnold

'ARCHIDUC JOSEPH'

As in a rose garden, so in a rose book: no matter how many roses you can include, there are so many other beauties silently pleading for admittance. The 100-odd we have met already would be enough to furnish an extensive garden – but here are brief introductions to another 150, grouped by the stations in life of the people whose names they bear.

They range across the full spectrum of rose types. Some are of high antiquity, others so new they have only just appeared in the catalogues; but each is beautiful and desirable, and all honour-worthy people. Their acquaintance is well worth making.

ROSES FOR WIVES AND MOTHERS

ANNE LETTS
Pale pink exhibition HT, George Letts (UK), 1954
'Named for the most wonderful woman I have ever known, my mother' and a leading show rose for many years.

ROSA ECAE
Bright yellow shrubby species from Afghanistan
Discovered in 1879 by a British soldier–botanist and named with his wife's initials – E.C.A. for Eleanor Carmichael Aitchison.

GRAND-MÈRE JENNY
Yellow and pink HT, Francis Meilland (France), 1950
The raiser's grandmother Jeanne Meilland (d. 1943), a farmer's wife who raised four children despite having lost a hand in an accident.

LADY PENZANCE
Copper-pink sweet briar hybrid, Lord Penzance (UK), 1894
Most of the Penzance briars have names taken from Walter Scott's novels, but the raiser reserved the two best for himself and his Lady.

LÉONIE LAMESCH
Scented orange-blend Polyantha, Peter Lambert (Germany), 1899
A charming wedding present from the raiser to his bride, the daughter of a leading German nurseryman.

MAMAN COCHET
Pink-blend tea, Scipion Cochet (France), 1892
One of the best-loved teas, dedicated by M. Cochet to his grandmother (Mme Pierre Cochet) for her 85th birthday.

'MAMAN COCHET'

MANOU MEILLAND
Deep pink HT, Meilland (France), 1979
Manou is the family's nickname for Louisette Meilland (née Paolino), widow of Francis Meilland and herself a rose breeder.

MME GEORGES DELBARD
Dark red HT, Delbard (France), 1980
Georges Delbard's tribute to his wife has for many years been the world's leading red flower-shop rose.

MME VICTOR VERDIER
Fragrant cherry-red HP, Eugène Verdier (France), 1863
As a contemporary journalist wrote, 'M. Verdier could not have chosen a worthier name for this magnificent rose than that of his mother.'

PAT AUSTIN
Fragrant copper and apricot shrub rose, David Austin (UK), 1995
'Lilian Austin' honours the raiser's mother, this one his wife, who is a talented sculptor.

SALLY HOLMES
Ivory and peach shrub rose, Robert Holmes (UK), 1976
It is said the raiser refused to patent this superb rose so his tribute to his wife would be unsullied by considerations of profit.

SARAH VAN FLEET
Fragrant clear pink rugosa, Walter van Fleet (USA), 1926
Sarah Heilman had been the raiser's childhood sweetheart, but for some reason his beautiful tribute to her was not introduced until after his death.

ROSES FOR THE FAMILY

ALEC'S RED
Fragrant cherry-red HT, Alec Cocker (UK), 1970
The raiser's first success, introduced under the nickname given during its trials by his admiring colleagues.

AVANDEL
Peaches and cream miniature, Ralph Moore (USA), 1977
The vaguely Arthurian name derives from the names of Mr Moore's wife, Ann, and his sisters Ava and Della.

AIMÉE VIBERT
White noisette, Jean-Pierre Vibert (France), 1826
'So beautiful I gave it the name of my darling daughter.' Aimée was also Vibert's mother's name.

CHARLES AUSTIN
Apricot/yellow shrub rose, David Austin (UK), 1973
Named for the raiser's father, a Norfolk farmer who initially looked askance at his son's decision to specialise in roses.

GRANDPA DICKSON
('Irish Gold') Pale yellow exhibition HT, Pat Dickson (UK), 1966
The raiser's father Alex Dickson (1893–1975), known in the family as Grandpa and himself a notable raiser of roses.

JAYNE AUSTIN
Fragrant peaches and cream shrub rose, David Austin (UK), 1993
Named for the raiser's daughter-in-law and thought by many to be the best peach-to-apricot rose he has raised. It is a very tall grower.

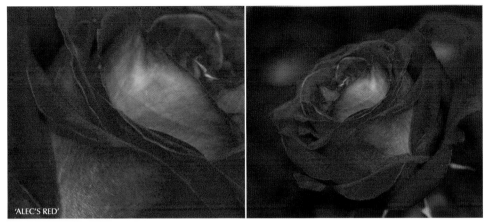

'ALEC'S RED'

Yvonne Arnold

L.D. BRAITHWAITE
Scented red shrub rose, David Austin (UK), 1988
The raiser's father-in-law, Leonard Dudley Braithwaite, is honoured by an excellent easy-to-grow rose.

MICHÈLE MEILLAND
Blush and peach HT, Francis Meilland (France), 1945
The raiser's daughter, nicknamed Michou, now Mme Raymond Richardier. She has created many recent Meilland roses.

ROSE GAUJARD
Cyclamen and white HT, Jean Gaujard (France), 1957
'M. Jean Gaujard thought so highly of this rose he named it after himself.' It remains his best-known rose.

SONIA
Salmon-pink HT, Alain Meilland (France), 1974
The world's most popular flower-shop rose for many years is named for Alain and Nadine Meilland's daughter, born in 1968.

SOPHIE'S PERPETUAL
Pink-blend china rose, Humphrey Brooke (UK), 1960
Brooke found this old rose in the garden of his wife's grandmother Countess Sophie von Benkendorff (1857–1928) and gave it her name.

ROSES FOR KEEN GARDENERS

GARTENDIREKTOR OTTO LINNE
Pink cluster-flowered shrub, Peter Lambert (Germany), 1934
The rose-loving Otto Linne (1869–1937) was Hamburg's Director of Parks and Gardens and designed several of that city's parks.

JEAN KENNEALLY
Apricot miniature, Dee Bennett (USA), 1984
Jean Unita Kenneally of San Diego (1907–2006) was one of America's leading rose exhibitors and show judges.

MME ALFRED CARRIÈRE
Fragrant white noisette, Joseph Schwartz (France), 1879
One of the finest climbing roses, 'dedicated to the wife of a great lover of roses from our own province of Dauphiné.'

MME ERNEST CALVAT
Fragrant soft pink bourbon, Veuve Schwartz (France), 1888
Marie Calvat, *née* Perrin (1859–96) and her husband (1852–1910) bred chrysanthemums in their garden in Grenoble.

MRS DUDLEY CROSS
Cream and pink tea, William Paul (UK), 1907
A favourite exhibition rose for many years, named for the wife of one of the leading British exhibitors of the day.

'MME ALFRED CARRIÈRE'

Paul Barden

MRS REYNOLDS HOLE
Fragrant pink tea, Gilbert Nabonnand (France), 1900
Caroline Hole (*née* Francklin) once said she loved flowers even more than her husband Dean Hole did – and he founded the National Rose Society!

SEXY REXY
Soft pink floribunda, Sam McGredy (New Zealand), 1984
Named in memory of a friend of the raiser – not, as sometimes claimed, for the actor Rex Harrison.

SOUVENIR D'ALPHONSE LAVALLÉE
Fragrant maroon HP, Charles Verdier (France), 1884
The dendrologist Alphonse Lavallée (1833–84) was President of the National Horticultural Society of France.

ROSA WILLMOTTIAE
Pink shrubby species from China, introduced 1904
Honours Ellen Willmott (1860–1934), a celebrated British gardener, author of the lavish monograph *The Genus Rosa*.

WILLIAM ALLEN RICHARDSON
Apricot to orange noisette, Veuve Ducher (France), 1878
Named by Mme Ducher for a faithful customer, a millionaire from Kentucky. It is a sport of his favourite rose, the pale yellow 'Rêve d'Or'.

ROSES FOR NURSERY PEOPLE

ADOLPH HORSTMANN
Yellow and apricot HT, Reimer Kordes (Germany), 1971
Named for an old family friend and near neighbour, the owner of the largest retail nursery in Europe.

CHARLES LAWSON
Fragrant mauve-pink bourbon hybrid, Lawson & Son (UK), 1853
The Edinburgh nurseryman who also introduced the Lawson cypress (*Chamaecyperis lawsoniana*). A common 'found' rose.

DUPONTII
Fragrant blush-white shrub rose, André Dupont (France), 1813
M. Dupont advised the Empress Joséphine on her roses, and it is said she ordered this classic single rose should bear his own name.

EVELYN FISON
Scarlet floribunda, Sam McGredy (UK), 1962
Sponsored by Fisons Ltd, a British maker of horticultural products, and named for the chairman's wife. McGredy's pink-blend 'Priscilla Burton' (1978) honours the wife of a later chairman.

HENRY NEVARD
Fragrant dark red HP, Frank Cant (UK), 1924
Frank Cant's splendid tribute to his nursery foreman, one of the finest English rosarians of his day.

LOUISE ODIER
Fragrant pink bourbon, Jacques Margottin (France), 1851
The records don't say whether Louise was the wife or daughter of the Parisian horticulturist James Odier.

'SPEK'S YELLOW'

Yvonne Arnold

MME LAURIOL DE BARNY
Fragrant pink bourbon, Victor Trouillard (France), 1868
The daughter and heiress of the great nurseryman André Leroy of Angers (1801–75); her husband Edouard Loriol de Barny was mayor of Angers.

PAPA GONTIER
Fragrant carmine tea, Gilbert Nabonnand (France), 1882
Gontier père, nurseryman of Montrouge near Orléans, was famous for his skill at growing flowers and fruit under glass.

SOUVENIR DE MME LÉONIE VIENNOT
Fragrant shrimp-pink climbing tea, Pierre Bernaix (France), 1898
Named in memory of the wife of a colleague, Viennot of Dijon, one of the leading rose growers of the day.

SPEK'S YELLOW
Yellow HT, Jac Verschuren (Netherlands), 1947
A leading breeder of miniature roses, the Dutch hybridist Jan Spek introduced this rose, the leading yellow HT for many years.

THE DOCTOR
Huge fragrant pink HT, Fred Howard (USA), 1936
Dr Jean-Henri Nicolas (1875–1937) of Jackson & Perkins: scientist, soldier and Chevalier of the Legion of Honour. He coined the term 'floribunda'.

ULRICH BRUNNER
Fragrant cherry-red HP, Antoine Levet (France), 1881
Ulrich Brunner Fils (1848– ?) was a rose grower of Lausanne in Switzerland. Alas, he went bankrupt in 1891 and died in obscurity.

ROSES FOR THE ARISTOCRACY

MISS ALICE
Fragrant pink shrub rose, David Austin (UK), 2000
Alice de Rothschild (1847–1922), a friend of Queen Victoria and creator of the rose garden at Waddeston Manor in Buckinghamshire.

BOULE DE NANTEUIL
Fragrant purple gallica, Roesser (France), 1834
Named by the raiser for a prominent local family, that of the Counts Boula (not Boule) de Nanteuil.

COMTESSE DU CAŸLA
Fragrant copper and yellow china, Pierre Guillot (France), 1902
The most famous of several Comtesses du Caÿla was the beautiful but controversial Zöe Tallon (1785–1852), mistress of Louis XVIII.

DAME EDITH HELEN
Fragrant pink exhibition HT, Alex Dickson (UK), 1929
Edith, Marchioness of Londonderry (1878–1959) created the World Heritage nominated garden of Mount Stewart near Belfast.

DUCHESSE DE MONTEBELLO
Fragrant pink gallica, Jean Laffay (France), 1829
The beautiful Louise Antoinette (1782–1856), wife of Maréchal Lannes whom Napoleon created Duc de Montebello in 1808.

EUGÈNE DE BEAUHARNAIS
Fragrant purple-red china, Alexandre Hardy (France), 1837
A tribute from the raiser to the son of his old employer the Empress Joséphine. He lived from 1791 to 1824.

'LADY SYLVIA'

HUME'S BLUSH
Fragrant pale pink tea, Chinese origin, 1809
Lady Amelia Hume (1751–1810), whose husband Sir Abraham imported this first of the tea roses from China.

LADY SYLVIA
Fragrant pink HT, William Stevens (UK), 1926
The pink flower-shop rose for forty years, named for the beautiful (and much-married) actress and poet Sylvia, Lady Ashley (1904–77). She was Clark Gable's third wife.

PRINCE CAMILLE DE ROHAN
Fragrant dark red HP, Eugène Verdier (France), 1861
Camille-Philippe de Rohan (1801–92), Prince of Rohan and Guémené, was a keen gardener with a special interest in orchids.

PRINCE CHARLES
Fragrant purple bourbon, Alexandre Hardy (France), c.1842
Not the present Prince of Wales but Napoleon's nephew Charles-Lucien Bonaparte (1803–57), Prince of Canino.

ROBERT LE DIABLE
Fragrant purple centifolia, raiser unknown (France), c.1835
The hero of Meyerbeer's grand opera of 1831, Robert le Diable, based very loosely on the life of Robert, Duke of Normandy (c.1010–35).

SHARIFA ASMA
Fragrant pale pink shrub rose, David Austin (UK), 1989
The dedication of this rose was a birthday present from an Arab prince to his rose-loving wife.

ROSES FOR ROYALTY

DUCHESSE D'ANGOULÊME
Fragrant shell-pink gallica, Jean-Pierre Vibert (France), c.1827
Daughter of Louis XVI and Marie Antoinette, Marie Thérèse Charlotte d'Angoulême escaped the Revolution but died in exile in 1851.

DUKE OF EDINBURGH
Fragrant dark red HP, William Paul (UK), 1868
Queen Victoria's music-loving second son Alfred Duke of Edinburgh (1844–1900), the first member of the royal family to visit Australia.

DUKE OF WINDSOR
Fragrant orange-red HT, Matthias Tantau (Germany), 1968
It is said that when the name was proposed the garden-loving former King Edward VIII exclaimed, 'I thought they only named roses after ladies!'

KAISERIN AUGUSTE VIKTORIA
Fragrant white HT, Peter Lambert (Germany), 1891
The art- and music-loving Auguste Viktoria of Schleswig-Holstein (1858–1921). She married Kaiser Wilhelm II of Germany in 1881.

MARIE LOUISE
Fragrant pink damask, raiser unknown, c.1813
Raised at Malmaison and dedicated as a courtesy to Napoleon's second wife, Marie Louise of Austria (1791–1847).

'QUEEN NEFERTITI'

Yvonne Arnold

MARY QUEEN OF SCOTS
Purple spinosissima, raiser unknown, c.1820
A fine Scotch rose to remember the beautiful and tragic Mary Stuart (1542–87). She was a poet and a lover of flowers.

NUR MAHAL
Fragrant muted red hybrid musk, Joseph Pemberton (UK), 1923
The all-powerful wife of the Emperor Jahangir of India, who credited her with inventing attar of roses. The Taj Mahal entombs her niece Mumtaz Mahal.

PRINCESS ALICE
('Zonta Rose') Yellow floribunda, Jack Harkness (UK), 1985
Princess Alice, Duchess of Gloucester (1901–2004) was a keen rose lover. The other name honours the women's organisation Zonta International.

PRINCESSE DE QATAR
Red HT, Arnaud Delbard (France), 2006
Her Highness Sheikha Mozah is UNESCO's special envoy for basic and higher education.

QUEEN NEFERTITI
Peach and yellow shrub, David Austin (UK), 1988
The famously beautiful consort of the Pharaoh and religious reformer Akhnaten (reigned 1351–34 BCE). She appears in Philip Glass's opera Akhnaten, premiered in 1984.

VICTOR EMMANUEL
Fragrant dark purple bourbon, Jean-Baptiste Guillot (France), 1859
One of the richest of all regal purple roses, for Victor Emmanuel II (1820–78), the first king of the united Italy.

ROSES FOR STATESMEN AND LEADERS

D'AGUESSEAU
Crimson gallica, Jean-Pierre Vibert (France), 1836
As Chancellor of France, Henri d'Aguesseau (1668–1751) achieved major reform of the French legal system. He was a keen gardener.

JOHN F. KENNEDY
Fragrant white HT, Jackson & Perkins (USA), 1965
When J&P proposed dedicating a rose to President Kennedy's memory, his widow Jacqueline requested it be white.

K OF K
Single crimson HT, Alex Dickson (UK), 1917
The army's nickname for Horatio Kitchener, Earl Kitchener of Khartoum (1850–1916), British field-marshal and statesman.

LADY CURZON
Fragrant pink shrub rose, Charles Turner (UK), 1901
Mary Leitner (d. 1908), the beautiful American-born wife of George, Baron Curzon (1859–1925), Viceroy of India.

MARGARET THATCHER
(KORflüg) Pink HT, Reimer Kordes (Germany), 1979
Margaret, Baroness Thatcher (1925–), British Prime Minister from 1979 to 1990. Her rose is also known as 'Flamingo'!

MME EDOUARD HERRIOT
('The Daily Mail Rose') Coral HT, Joseph Pernet-Ducher (France), 1913
Blanche Herriot (née Rabatel, 1877–1962) was a friend of the raiser. Her husband was mayor of Lyon and three times Premier of France.

'LADY CURZON'

PRESIDENT HERBERT HOOVER
Fragrant pink and gold HT, L.B. Coddington (USA), 1930
Named to celebrate the election of Herbert Clark Hoover (1874–1964) as 31st President of
the USA.

RONALD REAGAN
Red/purple and white HT, Keith Zary (USA), 2005
Named in memory of the actor who became President of the USA, 'the first red white and blue
rose' is really red and white, fading to purple.

SIR WINSTON CHURCHILL
Fragrant pink HT, Alex Dickson (UK), 1955
The great wartime British Prime Minister (1874–1965) was a keen rose lover and it's a pity his rose
is rarely seen now.

ROSES FOR WRITERS

ANAÏS SÉGALAS
Fragrant mauve gallica, Jean-Pierre Vibert (France), 1837
By the age of twenty-three Anaïs Ségalas (1814–93) had already published two widely acclaimed volumes of poetry.

CHAUCER
Fragrant pink shrub rose, David Austin (UK), 1970
The father of English literature, Geoffrey Chaucer (1342–1400). Austin has named several roses after characters from Chaucer's *Canterbury Tales*.

CONRAD FERDINAND MEYER
Fragrant pink rugosa hybrid, Franz Müller (Germany), 1899
The Swiss novelist and poet (1825–98), who was famed for the marmoreal perfection of his verse.

EDITOR MCFARLAND
Fragrant rose-pink HT, Charles Mallerin (France), 1931
Author of several books on roses, J. Horace McFarland (d.1948) was Editor of the *American Rose Annual* for nearly thirty years.

FRÉDÉRIC MISTRAL
(MEltebros, 'The Children's Rose') Fragrant soft pink HT, Meilland (France), 1995
Named in memory of the rose-loving Provençal poet (1830–1914), winner of the 1904 Nobel Prize for Literature.

HANS CHRISTIAN ANDERSEN
Dark red floribunda, Pernille Olesen (Denmark), 1986
Though he never had a garden of his own, Andersen (1805–75) loved roses, which often feature in his fairytales.

'SUSAN HAMPSHIRE'

HOMÈRE
Fragrant cream and pink tea, Robert & Moreau (France), 1858
The incomparable Greek poet Homer, to whom *The Iliad* and *The Odyssey* have been ascribed since antiquity.

KAREN BLIXEN
Scented white HT, Pernille Olesen (Denmark), 1995
The Danish Baroness Blixen (1885–1962), whose pen-name was Isak Dinesen. Her best-known work is *Out of Africa.*

MARCHESA BOCCELLA
Fragrant pink Portland, Desprez (France), c.1840
The Florentine Marchesa Cesare Boccella was a friend of Franz Liszt, who set one of her poems to music in 1842.

NUITS DE YOUNG
('The Old Black Moss') Fragrant maroon moss, Jean Laffay (France), 1845
Edward Young (1683–1765), whose 1742 epic poem *Night Thoughts* enjoyed great popularity (in translation) in mid-nineteenth-century France.

SAINT-EXUPÉRY
Mauve HT, Georges Delbard (France), 1961
The novelist and airman Antoine de Saint-Exupéry (1900–44). Its better-known seedling 'Vol de Nuit' honours his best-known novel.

SUSAN HAMPSHIRE
Rose-pink HT, Alain Meilland (France), 1972
The British TV star (b. 1942) is also well known as a novelist and author of books on gardening.

ROSES FOR ARTISTS

CHARLES RENNIE MACKINTOSH
Lilac-pink shrub rose, David Austin (UK), 1988
The great Scottish architect and designer (1868–1928) often included stylised roses in his designs.

CHIHULY
Multicoloured floribunda, Tom Carruth (USA), 2004
The American glass artist Dale Chihuly (1941–), many of whose sculptures are inspired by, and displayed in, gardens.

CHRISTIAN DIOR
Red exhibition HT, Francis Meilland (France), 1958
A supremely elegant rose for the Paris couturier (1905–57) whose name has become a byword for elegance.

EMANUEL
Fragrant pale pink shrub rose, David Austin (UK), 1985
A huge silken flower for the British couturier Elizabeth Emanuel, who created Princess Diana's wedding dress in 1981.

HENRI MATISSE
Red and white striped HT, Arnaud Delbard (France), 1995
The great post-impressionist painter (1869–1954) loved the bright reds and pinks that this rose displays.

LEONARDO DA VINCI
Fragrant pink floribunda, Meilland (France), 1994
The raisers say the flowers remind them of those of the time of the great Renaissance painter, inventor and all-round genius.

'SONIA RYKIEL'

MICHELANGELO
Fragrant yellow HT, Meilland (France), 1997
Named to celebrate the restoration of the glorious Sistine Chapel frescoes of Michelangelo Buonarotti (1475–1564).

REDOUTÉ
Fragrant pale pink shrub rose, David Austin (UK), 1992
'The Raphael of the rose', Pierre-Joseph Redouté (1759–1840) ranks among the greatest of all botanical artists.

RUBENS
Fragrant blush-pink tea, Moreau & Robert (France), 1859
The Flemish painter and diplomat Sir Peter Paul Rubens (1577–1640) was famous for the subtlety of his flesh tones.

SONIA RYKIEL
Fragrant pink shrub rose, Dominique Massad (France), 1995
The Paris couturier (born 1930), whose casual but ultra-elegant clothes have been shown at the Louvre.

TITIAN
Cerise-red shrub rose, Frank Riethmuller (Australia), 1950
Its glowing colour reminded the raiser of the rich canvases of his favourite painter, who lived from 1488 to 1576.

ROSES FOR MUSICIANS

BENJAMIN BRITTEN
Fragrant coral red shrub rose, David Austin (UK), 2001
Pianist, conductor and the greatest British composer of his time, Benjamin Britten (1913–76) was a rose lover.

BARBRA STREISAND
Fragrant mauve HT, Tom Carruth (USA),1999
Chosen by the rose-loving singer and Academy Award-winning actress herself to bear her name.

DOLLY PARTON
Fragrant orange-red HT, Joseph Winchel (USA),1985
A big, bright rose for the voluptuous blonde country-and-western singer, born in 1946.

JACQUELINE DU PRÉ
Fragrant off-white shrub rose, Jack Harkness (UK),1988
A compact and very pretty shrub named in memory of the celebrated British cellist (1945–87).

KATHLEEN FERRIER
Fragrant pink floribunda/shrub rose, Buisman (Holland), 1952
A little known but excellent rose for the great and greatly loved British contralto (1912–1953), who was very popular in Holland.

MARIA CALLAS
('Miss All-American Beauty') Fragrant deep pink HT, Alain Meilland (France), 1963
The Greek-American soprano (1923–77), famous alike for her wonderful singing and her fiery temperament.

'SADLER'S WELLS'

Yvonne Arnold

MOZART
Deep pink and white shrub rose, Peter Lambert (Germany), 1937
Hardly as famous as its namesake Wolfgang Amadeus Mozart (1756–91), but a fine rose.

NANA MOUSKOURI
Fragrant white floribunda, Pat Dickson (UK), 1975
A white rose for the popular Greek singer (1934–) whose signature tune is 'White Roses from Athens'.

SADLER'S WELLS
Pink and red blend shrub rose, Peter Beales (UK), 1983
A tribute to the dancers and musicians of the Royal Ballet and their home theatre, Sadler's Wells in London.

PERGOLÈSE
Fragrant mauve-pink portland, Robert & Moreau (France), 1860
The composer Giovanni Battista Pergolesi (1710–36), whose 'Stabat Mater' enjoyed great popularity in the nineteenth century.

SOUVENIR DE LOUIS AMADE
Fragrant pink HT, Arnaud Delbard (France), 2000
Louis Amade (1915–92), the Paris police chief who wrote the lyrics of some of Edith Piaf's and Gilbert Bécaud's best loved songs.

WILLIAM CHRISTIE
Fragrant pink shrub rose, Dominique Massad (France), 1998
A suitably old-fashioned flower for the American–French conductor (1944–), a leading interpreter of the music of the seventeenth and eighteenth centuries.

ROSES FOR THE STARS

AUDREY HEPBURN
Soft pink HT, Gerry Twomey (USA), 1988
An elegant rose for the elegant star, a tireless worker for UNESCO and a life-long lover of the rose.

CATHERINE DENEUVE
Fragrant warm pink HT, Meilland (France), 1981
Named to celebrate the beautiful Mlle Deneuve's César award (the French Oscar) for best actress in *Le Dernier Métro*.

ELIE SEMOUN
Dark red floribunda with variegated leaves, Delbard (France), 2007
The insouciant variegated leaves suggested the dedication to the popular French comedian, actor and singer, an ardent garden lover.

ELIZABETH TAYLOR
Fragrant, smoky deep pink HT, Weddel (USA), 1985
The beautiful Miss Taylor is famous for her many movies, her many marriages and her work for AIDS victims.

GENE TIERNEY
Soft yellow shrub rose, Guillot (France), 1999
The beautiful Miss Tierney (1920–91) is best known for her roles in *Laura* and *The Ghost and Mrs Muir*.

GINA LOLLOBRIGIDA
Fragrant golden-yellow HT, Meilland (France), 1997
An appropriately shapely flower for the voluptuous Italian actress, born in 1927.

'CATHERINE DENEUVE'

INGRID BERGMAN
Bright red HT, Poulsen (Denmark), 1984
Named in memory of the great and controversial Swedish actress, three times Academy Award winner.

JAMES MASON
Rich red gallica hybrid, Peter Beales (England), 1982
The British actor and producer (1909–84) was a keen rose lover. The apricot miniature 'Clarissa' (Harkness, 1982) honours his wife Clarissa Kaye-Mason.

MARILYN MONROE
Pale apricot HT, Tom Carruth (USA), 2002
A shapely 'blonde' rose for one of the icons of the cinema, who died tragically in 1963.

PETER FRANKENFELD
Deep pink HT, Reimer Kordes (Germany), 1966
The raiser was a fan of the German radio and television presenter and comedian Peter Frankenfeld (1913–79).

VIOLET CARSON
Salmon pink floribunda, Sam McGredy (UK), 1963
Best known as Ena Sharples in *Coronation Street*, Violet Carson OBE (1898–1983) was a keen rose lover in real life.

ROSES FOR HOLY PEOPLE

ARRILLAGA
Fragrant pale pink HP, Father George Schoener (USA), 1929
The pious Don José de Arrillaga (1750–1814), Governor of Spanish California and like the raiser a member of the Order of St Francis.

CARDINAL HUME
Fragrant purple shrub rose, Jack Harkness (UK), 1984
The similarity of its colour to that of 'Cardinal de Richelieu' prompted the dedication to Basil Cardinal Hume (1923–99), Archbishop of Westminster.

ROSA DAVIDII
Pink shrubby species from western China, introduced 1908
Abbé Armand David (1826–1900), a French missionary in China who studied the flora and fauna of that country.

THE HOLY ROSE
Fragrant pale pink gallica hybrid, origin unknown
An ancient rose grown for centuries by Ethiopian monks as a holy relic of their founder St Frumentius, who brought it from Egypt in AD 326.

ROSA HUGONIS
(Father Hugo's Rose) Yellow shrubby species from China
Hugh (Hugo) Scallon (1851–1928) was an Irish Franciscan missionary in China. He sent seed of this rose to Kew in 1899.

MARY MCKILLOP
Fragrant pink floribunda, Armstrong (USA), 1989
Blessed Mary McKillop (1842–1909), the South Australian nun who devoted her life to educating poor outback children.

ST CECILIA
Fragrant cream shrub rose, David Austin (UK), 1987
The semi-legendary third century martyr who has been the patron saint of music since the sixteenth century.

ST FRANCIS XAVIER
Scented crimson HT, George Thomson (Australia), 2006
Named to honour the great Jesuit missionary's 500th birthday, which was also the sesquicentenary of his cathedral in Adelaide, South Australia.

ST PATRICK
Yellow HT, Frank Strickland (USA), 1996
The flowers are often strongly tinted green, hence the dedication to the patron saint of Ireland.

SOUVENIR DE ST ANNE'S
Fragrant pink bourbon, introduced by Hilling (UK), 1950
St Anne's (from the Holy Well of St Anne on its grounds) is the Dublin garden where this sport of 'Souvenir de la Malmaison' arose.

ROSES FOR HEROES AND HEROINES

ADMIRAL RODNEY
Fragrant pink exhibition HT, C. Trew (UK), 1973
George Brydges Rodney (1718–92), whose victory at the Battle of the Saints in 1782 broke French power in the Caribbean.

AVIATEUR BLÉRIOT
Fragrant peach-yellow rambler, Fauque & Fils (France), 1910
Louis Blériot (1872–1936) made the first international aeroplane flight (from Calais to Dover) in 1909.

ALEXANDER
Orange-red HT, Jack Harkness (UK), 1972
Named in memory of Field-Marshall Earl Alexander of Tunis (1891–1969) under whom the raiser served in World War II.

BELLE STORY
Fragrant pink shrub rose, David Austin (UK), 1984
She was one of the first three nursing sisters to serve on board the ships of the Royal Navy, in 1884.

CHARLES DARWIN
Yellow shrub rose, David Austin (UK), 2001
The biologist whose discoveries changed science forever was born in 1809 not far from where the raiser has his nurseries.

GÉNÉRAL KLÉBER
Fragrant pink moss, Moreau & Robert (France), 1856
Born in 1753, Jean-Baptiste Kléber was appointed administrator of Egypt by Napoleon. He was assassinated in Cairo in 1800.

'OPHELIA'

Yvonne Arnold

GRACE DARLING
Fragrant cream and pink HT, Henry Bennett (UK), 1884
During a terrible storm, Grace Darling (1815–42) rescued nine survivors from a ship wrecked near her father's lighthouse.

EGLANTYNE
Fragrant pale pink shrub rose, David Austin (UK), 1994
Moved by the horrors of World War I, Eglantyne Jebb (1876–1928) founded the International Save the Children Fund in 1920.

JACQUES CARTIER
Fragrant pink portland, Moreau & Robert (France), 1868
The Breton explorer (1491–1557), discoverer of the St Lawrence River in Canada in 1534.

OPHELIA
Fragrant pale pink HT, William Paul (UK), 1912
Of Paul's two Shakespearean roses of 1912, the red-and-yellow 'Juliet' has long gone from the catalogues, but 'Ophelia' (from *Hamlet*) remains a classic.

PENELOPE
Fragrant blush hybrid musk, Joseph Pemberton (UK), 1924
The best-known of several roses dedicated to the sorely tried but faithful heroine of Homer's *The Odyssey*.

ROSES FOR AUSTRALIANS

APRIL HAMER
Fragrant pink-blend exhibition HT, Ron Bell (Australia), 1983
A patron of the arts, Lady Hamer (née Mackintosh) is the widow of Sir Rupert Hamer, Premier of Victoria from 1972 to 1981.

COUNTESS OF STRADBROKE
Fragrant red climbing HT, Alister Clark (Australia), 1928
Henrietta Violet, Countess of Stradbroke (d. 1947) whose husband the third Earl was Governor of Victoria from 1921 to 1926.

GINGER MEGGS
Orange floribunda, Mathias Tantau (Germany), 1962
The red-headed urchin of Australia's favourite comic strip, originally created by Jimmy Bancks in 1921.

GREG CHAPPELL
Apricot HT, Armstrong Nurseries (USA), 1984
The cricketer who played 87 test matches for Australia, 47 of them as captain. He is a keen organic gardener.

HOWARD FLOREY
Fragrant apricot floribunda, George Thomson (Australia), 2002
'Australia's greatest scientist', Sir Howard (1898–1968) won the Nobel Prize for his development of penicillin.

'LADY HUNTINGFIELD'

IAN THORPE
Russet and cream HT, Wyn and Huibert Olij (Holland), 1997
Named for the Olympic swimming champion (1982–) to aid his work for underprivileged children.

LADY HUNTINGFIELD
Fragrant amber-yellow HT, Alister Clark (Australia), 1937
Margaret Eleanor (née Crosby), wife of Baron Huntingfield, the then Governor of Victoria and later Acting Governor-General. She died in 1943.

NANCY HAYWARD
Cerise climber, Alister Clark (Australia), 1937
Named (it is said, without her permission) for the daughter of a rose-loving friend of the raiser, Victorian Chief Justice Sir William Irvine.

TRACEY WICKHAM
Yellow and red miniature, Eric Welsh (Australia), 1984
A very fine rose to honour the young swimmer who won gold at the Commonwealth Games in 1978 and 1982.

HOW TO GROW
ROSES

It is the time you have spared for your rose that makes your rose so important

Antoine de Saint-Exupéry

One sometimes hears that the pace of modern life is so hectic that people have little time for gardening any more. 'Low maintenance' is to be the watchword for the gardens of the twenty-first century; and roses (it is alleged) are just too difficult and time-consuming.

Not so. Queen of Flowers the rose may be, but it would hardly be the world-wide favourite it is if it were temperamental and difficult to please. Sure, it isn't a 'plant it and forget it' plant, but the little attentions they demand are part of the pleasure of growing roses – and no plant rewards you more for them.

Give them sunshine

The ideal is unobstructed sunlight all day at all seasons, but at any rate at least half a day's worth. Plant a rose where it gets less and it may survive, but it will always be weak and sickly no matter how generously you water and fertilise it.

Don't forget, however, that climbing roses can often be placed where they can reach up into the sunlight, and in city gardens they are often the roses of choice. (They need to be tied to a trellis of some sort.)

An apparent contradiction: in hot-summer climates many roses appreciate a little shelter from the hottest afternoon sun which can scorch or fade the flowers, especially of the dark reds and the orange tones. These will appreciate an easterly aspect, or a place where distant trees will break the western sun. But they still need half a day's sunshine.

'LAMARQUE'

Don't stint on the manure

Roses don't mind whether your soil be light or heavy, mildly acid or mildly alkaline so long as drainage is good; but they insist on it being as rich as Christmas cake.

Prepare their beds generously, digging them over to a spade's depth, then spreading as thick a layer of manure as possible and fork it into the soil. Ten centimetres (4 inches) is not too much. This should be done about six weeks before you're due to plant so the manure has time to mellow; fresh manure can burn the new roots. By all means supplement it with home-made compost.

Tradition holds that cow manure is the rose's favourite – but any available sort will do, remembering that manure from birds, such as poultry manure, is more concentrated than that from mammals like cows, horses and sheep.

Then give the roses a mulch of the same every winter after you've finished pruning (thick enough to mask the soil completely), topping it up with straw, lucerne hay or whatever, but not wood or bark chips which provide no nourishment. Roses love being mulched, both for nourishment and to keep their roots cool.

The lesson I have learnt, and wish to pass on to others, is to know
the enduring happiness that the love of a garden gives.

Gertrude Jekyll

245

Don't crowd them

Roses love fresh air circulating through their branches; bugs and fungus diseases hate it.

The rule of thumb in mild climates is to set bush roses (hybrid teas and floribundas) a metre apart, a little more for more vigorous varieties. The taller growers go at the back of the bed, of course. Hybrid perpetuals and teas are usually big bushes and can go in at about 1.2 metres spacing. Shrub roses and climbers are spaced according to size: shrubs from 1.5 to 2 metres apart, climbers on a wall or fence from 2.5 to 4 metres apart according to vigour. (Always set a climber about 30 centimetres from the wall or fence or you won't be able to weed behind it.)

At that spacing you can carpet your beds with pansies, but if you plan to grow taller flowers among your roses you will need to allow plenty of room for them lest they crowd the roses. The choice of companion flowers is yours. Blue flowers always look wonderful with roses, but feel free to mix and match as your imagination suggests.

'ROSA MUNDI'

Yvonne Arnold

Buy top-quality plants

The best come from specialist rose-growers with reputations to maintain, but you can buy good plants at the local garden centre – even at chain stores, though roses have a short shelf-life indoors and you must be sure they are fresh. Roses are traditionally sold bare-rooted, that is, having been lifted from the soil and presented with damp straw or sawdust around their roots, often with plastic wrapping around that to keep everything moist. Look for a well-developed root system and plump branches; avoid any with shrivelled bark, a sign they have been allowed to dry out.

Bare-root roses are planted from the end of May till August in the southern hemisphere, from about November to March in the northern. Many garden centres offer pot-grown roses in bloom from spring to autumn, which allows you to see the flowers before you buy, though the selection is usually limited. Points to look for here are an adequate-sized pot and strong growth with disease-free foliage. Avoid any plants that appear to have been allowed to dry out or are getting etiolated from being kept indoors.

Plant with care

Give your plants a good start. Bare-root roses, once unwrapped, should be carried around in a bucket of water. If the roots dry out they may never recover. If the roots are tangled, spread them out, and open a hole wide enough to take them without cramping and deep enough that the bud union (where the branches spring from the rootstock) will be at soil level. Make a mound of soil at the bottom, spread the roots out and down over it and half-fill the hole with soil. Tip in a bucket of water to settle the soil around the roots, and when it has drained away fill the rest of the soil in, water lightly, and spread a mulch. Unless the winter is unusually dry there should be no need for more water till growth begins.

Standard roses need a permanent stake, no smaller than 3 centimetres square hardwood. It's best put in place before you plant the rose, which is planted at roughly the depth it was in the nursery – you can see this by the soil mark on the stem. Tie it to its stake at once, with a single main tie (a strip of old cloth is better than string) just below the branches. Check this from time to time to make sure it isn't getting too tight and strangling the stem.

Keep the plants growing

No rose actually flowers continuously the way a petunia does. It grows, flowers, and then starts growing again. Repeat-blooming roses flower at the end of each cycle of growth, spring-only ones only on the first. How many cycles and 'flushes' of bloom you get depends on the length of your growing season. In Britain they get two, in summer and autumn; in Australia we expect four or even five.

Water deeply once a week during dry weather. (Dry soil encourages mildew.) Morning is the best time; if the leaves stay wet for more than a couple of hours, it encourages black spot. Trickle-irrigation or an upside-down soaker hose suits roses just fine, and the mechanics can be hidden under the mulch. If the mulch begins to thin out, top it up: remember, roses love their roots to be cool. And keep the beds weeded: weeds are great robbers of water and nourishment and they can provide cover for bugs.

If you're in the habit of walking on your rose beds to admire the flowers and tend the bushes, the surface soil may have caked under your weight, despite the mulch. A light hoeing mid-season will loosen it and let the air get to the roots again.

Trim off the spent flowers to save wasting the plant's energy on unwanted seed and as each flush fades you can give a deep watering and a shot of quick-acting fertiliser to boost the new cycle of growth. Use organic fertiliser for preference: blood-and-bone, seaweed or fish emulsion, or one of the new organic-based rose fertilisers, which should have a high potassium content. Potassium (K) boosts disease resistance.

If drought strikes and watering is not permissible, do none of these things – you don't want to encourage new growth when there is insufficient moisture in the soil to support it. The plants will ride the drought out by going into semi-dormancy. They'll probably look miserable, but they'll come back to life when the rain returns.

Sometime in early summer strong sappy shoots called water-shoots or basal growths arise from low down on the plant. On a repeat-blooming rose they are crowned with a candelabrum of flowers. On a spring-only one (and on most climbers) they don't flower in their first year. Cherish them and don't mistake them for suckers from the rootstock. These suckers can take over the whole bush and must be ripped (not cut) off as soon as you recognise them by their coming from below the bud union and by their different leaves and thorns.

Prune gently

Come winter, it's time to think about pruning – a much simpler task than it looks on paper. The rose grows by constantly renewing itself: as old branches decline and die, new ones grow to take their place. All you are doing is assisting in that process and keeping the plant young. In the southern hemisphere you can prune at any time from mid June till early August; in the northern the custom is to wait till the worst of the winter is over.

Before you start, make sure your secateurs are sharp enough to cut the stems cleanly, not tear them apart. Start by removing any dead branches. Then take out any that are obviously worn out, with thick grey bark and side shoots that are obviously too weak to bear decent flowers again. Cut them back to a strong young branch – and if you can't find any, take them off right to the base of the plant. That will leave you with branches three or four years old or younger; these you trim back by about a third, cutting to the growth buds which you'll find at the base of each leaf (or where a leaf has fallen).

The system is modified a little in the case of climbers and the spring-only shrub roses, as any long branches that haven't flowered yet only need to have their skinny ends removed. The spring-only shrubs – the gallicas and their ilk and most of the wild roses – can be given their initial thinning-out immediately after bloom, unless you expect hips.

When you've finished pruning, trim off any remaining old leaves, gather up the debris and burn it or send it to the tip. (Rose prunings make prickly compost, and most backyard compost heaps don't get hot enough to kill off disease spores.) Then it's time for the post-pruning spray to clear up any lingering bugs and give the plants a clean start for the new season. Even if you don't spray otherwise, this one is well worth doing. The traditional sprays are lime sulphur, white oil or cupric hydroxide – but choose one only and don't mix anything with it.

Then you can stir the remains of last year's mulch into the soil and spread a new one. I like to sprinkle around a little potassium sulphate and magnesium sulphate (Epsom salts) – about a teaspoon of each per plant – at this time. Both magnesium and potassium help boost disease resistance.

Don't get obsessive about bugs

Sap-sucking insects, chewing insects, fungi – the list of enemies lying in wait for your roses makes depressing reading, and the glib advice that all will be well if you only spray the bushes with an insecticide/fungicide cocktail every ten days is enough to put you off roses forever. Quite apart from the harm that pesticides can do to the environment, spraying is a time-consuming chore.

But take heart. If a rose is getting all the sun, air, moisture and nourishment it needs, it will be able to shake off its troubles with little assistance from you beyond the annual post-pruning clean-up spray. Roses are pretty tough.

Always check a rose's reputation for disease resistance in your area – especially to mildew in dry-summer climates, to black spot in muggy-summer ones – but if you can't resist a particular rose, try it anyway. If it proves hopelessly susceptible to mildew or black spot, you can always throw it out.

As a general rule, fragrant dark red roses are (alas) the most likely to get mildew, modern yellow ones black spot. The rugosas are the most disease-resistant group, and the teas and noisettes are almost all strongly resistant to black spot, making them first choice in humid sub-tropical areas.

Insects are easier to deal with. If you regularly inspect your roses, you'll be able to catch the first aphids or caterpillars and squash them. That often stops the invasion in its tracks.

If you find yourself in the middle of a major attack and must spray, choose the chemical currently recommended for the particular problem and spray until the attack is over. Then stop! Follow the directions to the letter, wear protective clothing, wash up immediately, and store concentrated chemicals (and fertilisers) safely out of reach of children and pets.

And don't get obsessive. A friend who had to give up spraying entirely a couple of years ago (doctor's orders to avoid any sort of toxic chemicals) reports that she gets no more black spot or mildew than when she sprayed every weekend. And within weeks of her stopping spraying, the singing birds and the ladybirds came to her garden to dine on the bugs.

'MARY MCKILLOP'

Don't leave all your roses in the garden

Though roses can be grown in pots (choose compact-growing varieties and give them substantial containers, no less than 15 litres for an average-sized rosebush, and be punctilious about watering), they do poorly as houseplants. But if you handle them properly, all roses will live out their full life in vases and bring beauty and scent to every room in the house – and joy to any friend to whom you give a bunch.

Cut them in the cool of the day, re-cut the stems under water, and stand them in deep tepid water almost to the base of the flowers for two or three hours before arranging them. (Wash the vase out with bleach before filling it with tepid water.) Strip any leaves that will be below the waterline, where they'll rot. Stripping the thorns makes arranging easier and is said to help the flowers last. Keep the arrangement in a cool place, out of direct sun and away from draughts.

Don't mutilate your plants for the sake of your vase. Don't take long stems from bushes in their first year, and after that always leave at least the two lowest leaves. With spring-only roses, you can cut whole flowering branches in anticipation of the post-flowering thinning-out. That is luxury!

> The blossoming of a single flower is a greater miracle
> than the raising of a man from the dead.
>
> *St Augustine*

251

GLOSSARY OF ROSE TYPES
Modern roses

BUSH ROSES

The most popular type of rose both in gardens and flower shops. They are divided into three groups:

Hybrid Tea (HT) with large flowers borne one or maybe three to a stem.

Examples: 'Helmut Schmidt', 'Helen Traubel', 'Mr Lincoln'

Floribunda with smaller flowers in clusters or sprays.

Examples: 'Lavender Pinocchio', 'Picasso',' Marjory Palmer'

Miniature with small flowers and leaves on a bush about 30 centimetres tall, like a hybrid tea seen through the wrong end of a telescope.

All three flower repeatedly and come in every colour but true blue.

SHRUB ROSES

These are a mixed bag, some resembling the wild roses in their growth (e.g. 'Basye's Purple'), others more like overgrown bush roses; but the term includes any rose whose informal habit makes it more suitable for consorting with perennials and other flowering shrubs than for massing in a formal roses-only bed. Some are sufficiently long-limbed to be treated as climbers.

Examples: 'Cara Bella', 'Graham Thomas', 'Bishop Darlington'

CLIMBING ROSES

A rose which makes branches long enough to train espalier-fashion on a trellis or pillar or over a pergola; most flowers are borne on the side-shoots. Flowers may resemble HTs or floribundas. Some bloom only in spring, others repeatedly, and size of plant varies.

Many are sports of the bush varieties whose names they bear, with the prefix 'Climbing' or its equivalent in other languages added. Their flowers are the same as those of the original bush variety, but they are not always borne very freely in summer and autumn.

Examples: 'Handel', 'Albertine', 'Climbing Lady Hillingdon'

RAMBLERS

These are climbers with small clustered flowers and slim, flexible branches. Most are spring-blooming only.

Examples: 'Dorothy Perkins', 'Ghislaine de Féligonde', 'Félicité et Perpétue'

Old Garden Roses (Heritage Roses)

Roses of any class which existed before 1867, irrespective of the date of the individual rose. They include:

SPRING-BLOOMING OLD ROSES

Gallicas and their close relatives the albas, damasks and centifolias, all of which make shrubby plants (the gallicas the most compact, the others taller) with many-petalled flat-faced flowers, usually very fragrant, in cool shades from white through pink to crimson and purple. They bloom in spring and do best in cool- to cold-winter climates.

Examples: 'Charles de Mills', 'Rosa Mundi', 'Mme Hardy'

MOSS ROSES

These roses have scented-moss-like outgrowths on the outside of the buds. Most are spring-only but some repeat.

Examples: 'Henri Martin', 'William Lobb', 'Chapeau de Napoléon'

REPEAT-BLOOMING OLD ROSES

China and tea roses resemble modern bush roses in habit, though slimmer in their branches and less hardy in severe-winter climates. The chinas are smallish in flower in shades of red and pink, the teas have large, nodding flowers mostly in pale shades from cream and soft yellow to pink and apricot. They are outstanding performers in warm, muggy climates. Climbing varieties are available.

Examples: 'Duchesse de Brabant', 'Lady Hillingdon', 'Mrs B.R. Cant'

BOURBON, PORTLAND AND HYBRID PERPETUAL ROSES

A rather mixed bag derived from crosses and inter-crosses with the gallica group and Chinas and teas. The portlands are the most compact, the hybrid perpetuals (HP) are the tallest and largest-flowered. Flower shape varies from gallica-like to HT-like; colours from white to dark crimson and purple. Some, especially among the HPs, often take a mid-summer holiday from flowering. Keep up the water, give them a shot of fertiliser, and they'll be back again in autumn.

Examples: 'Comte de Chambord', 'Général Jacqueminot', 'Mme Pierre Oger' (bourbon), 'Frau Karl Druschki'

NOISETTE ROSES

A mixed group of climbing roses, some cluster-flowered, most resembling climbing teas, in shades from white and palest pink to pale yellow and apricot. They mostly do best in warm-temperate to sub-tropical climates.

Examples: 'Blush Noisette', 'Lamarque', 'Maréchal Niel'

RUGOSA ROSES

Scented repeat-blooming shrubby roses derived from the Chinese and Japanese species *R. rugosa*. They are admired for their densely bushy growth and handsome foliage and hips.

Examples: 'Frau Dagmar Hastrup', 'Sarah Van Fleet'

Wild or Species Roses

The 150 or so species of the genus Rosa are found wild across the northern hemisphere. They have five-petalled flowers, almost always bloom only in spring, and range in habit from compact bushes to rampant climbers. Their fruits (hips) are often decorative.

Examples: *Rosa bracteata*, *Rosa moyesii*, *Rosa brunonii*

'ALISTER STELLA GRAY'

Yvonne Arnold

Acknowledgements

Anyone who writes on roses finds himself in good company, even when he walks a path as little trodden as the one that led to this book; and there are some people I must thank.

First, Yvonne Arnold in South Australia and Paul Barden in the United States, who not only photographed the roses specially for this book but suggested some favourites for inclusion.

Then, the rose lovers who delved into their albums for portraits of dedicatees and who generously shared their knowledge of them: Anja Merbach; Angela Pawsey of Cants of Colchester; Sam McGredy IV; Aline Converset of Meilland International; Stephanie Beyer; Helen Curtain of the Alister Clark Memorial Rose Garden; Professor David Byrne of Texas A&M University; Robert Siegel of Stanford University; and the picture librarians at the Rothschild Archives in London, the Royal National Rose Society, the National Portrait Gallery in London, and the State Library of Victoria. (Every effort has been made to contact the copyright holders of pictures and quotations: if you have missed out, please let the publishers know and we'll make corrections in future editions.)

Thanks too to Maureen and Andrew Ross and to Walter Duncan for providing Yvonne with roses not in her own collection; and to Lorilee Mallett, Jon Dodson, Ed Wilkinson and Jane Zammitt; and to Mark Graham who keeps my computer running smoothly. Their knowledge has greatly enriched mine; but any errors are entirely my own!

And to Jill Brown and her team at Random House: Chris Kunz the editor and the designers Christa Moffitt and Liz Seymour – and to my agent Averill Chase, who has supported this book since it was just a gleam in the author's eye.

Roger Mann has been a gardening writer for 20 years, including 10 years as gardening editor of the *Australian Family Circle* and ten as a regular contributor to *Your Garden*. He has written or co-written over 25 books on various gardening topics, including the best-selling *Yates Roses*.

Photographer Paul Barden lives in the United States and his hobby is breeding roses.

Photographer Yvonne Arnold lives in the Adelaide Hills where she has made one of Australia's finest rose gardens.

Extra photography credits

All the rose photographs have been taken by Yvonne Arnold and Paul Barden, with the exception of the following:

p.48   'Commandant Beaurepaire' © Mrs H. Evans
p.51   'Comte de Chambord' © Mrs H. Evans
p.89   'Général Galliéni' © Jocelen Janon
p.139   'Maurice Utrillo', lower right © Delbard
p.241   'Lady Huntingfield' © Jane Zammitt

Other image credits are as follows:

p. 2   Abraham Darby silhouette © Robert Siegel, Stanford University
p.14   Baronne Julie de Rothschild © Rothschild Archives
p.20   Robert Basye by courtesy of David H. Byrne © Texas A&M University
p.46   Charles Mallerin by courtesy of the Royal National Rose Society
p.58   Mary Donaldson © Getty Images
p.72   Edna Walling by courtesy of the State Library of Victoria
p.74   The Queen Mother by gracious permission of Her Majesty the Queen
p.76   Ellen Tofflemire by courtesy of Paul Barden
p.87   Herr and Frau Karl Druschki © Stephanie Beyer
p.90   Jean-François Jacqueminot by courtesy of the Library of Congress
p.92   Georg Arends © Anja Merbach
p.96   Graham Stuart Thomas © the Royal National Rose Society
p.108   Julia Clements © Julia Clements
p.110   Joanna Pawsey by courtesy of Cants of Colchester
p.118   Alice Lady Hillingdon © National Portrait Gallery
p.126   Lorraine Lee by courtesy of Helen Curtain
p.161   Ruth McGredy © Sam McGredy
p.166   Antoine Meilland by courtesy of Meilland
p.170   Meilland family © Meilland

'CONSTANCE SPRY'

Yvonne Arnold

An Ebury Press book
Published by Random House Australia Pty Ltd
Level 3, 100 Pacific Highway, North Sydney, NSW 2060
www.randomhouse.com.au

First published by Ebury Press in 2008

Addresses for companies within the Random House Group can be found at
www.randomhouse.com.au/offices

National Library of Australia
Cataloguing-in-Publication Entry

Mann, Roger, 1948–
Naming the rose.

ISBN 978 1 74166 830 8 (hbk.).

Roses.
Roses – Varieties
Rose culture

635.933734

Cover and internal design by Christabella Designs
Internal layout and typesetting by Seymour Designs
Printed and bound by Ibook

Random House Australia uses papers that are natural, renewable and recyclable products and
made from wood grown in sustainable forests. The logging and manufacturing processes are
expected to conform to the environmental regulations of the country of origin.

10 9 8 7 6 5 4 3 2 1